Applying Methods and Techniques of Futures Research

James L. Morrison, William L. Renfro,
Wayne I. Boucher, *Editors*

NEW DIRECTIONS FOR INSTITUTIONAL RESEARCH
Sponsored by the Association for Institutional Research
MARVIN W. PETERSON, *Editor-in-Chief*
PATRICK T. TERENZINI, *Associate Editor*

Number 39, September 1983

Paperback sourcebooks in
The Jossey-Bass Higher Education Series

Jossey-Bass Inc., Publishers
San Francisco • Washington • London

James L. Morrison, William L. Renfro, Wayne I. Boucher (Eds.).
Applying Methods and Techniques of Futures Research.
New Directions for Institutional Research, no. 39.
Volume X, number 3.
San Francisco: Jossey-Bass, 1983

New Directions for Institutional Research Series
Marvin W. Peterson, *Editor-in-Chief,* Patrick T. Terenzini, *Associate Editor*

New Directions for Institutional Research (publication number
USPS 098-830) is published quarterly by Jossey-Bass Inc.,
Publishers, and is sponsored by the Association for Institutional
Research. The volume and issue numbers above are included for
the convenience of libraries. Second-class postage rates paid at
San Francisco, California, and at additional mailing offices.

Correspondence:
Subscriptions, single-issue orders, change of address notices,
undelivered copies, and other correspondence should be sent to
New Directions Subscriptions, Jossey-Bass Inc., Publishers,
433 California Street, San Francisco, California 94104.

Editorial correspondence should be sent to the Editor-in-Chief,
Marvin W. Peterson, Center for the Study of Higher Education,
University of Michigan, Ann Arbor, Michigan 48109, or
Patrick T. Terenzini, Office of Institutional Research, SUNY,
Albany, New York 12222.

Library of Congress Catalogue Card Number LC 82-84194

International Standard Serial Number ISSN 0271-0579

International Standard Book Number ISBN 87589-957-9

Cover art by Willi Baum
Manufactured in the United States of America

Ordering Information

The paperback sourcebooks listed below are published quarterly and can be ordered either by subscription or single-copy.

Subscriptions cost $35.00 per year for institutions, agencies, and libraries. Individuals can subscribe at the special rate of $21.00 per year *if payment is by personal check.* (Note that the full rate of $35.00 applies if payment is by institutional check, even if the subscription is designated for an individual.) Standing orders are accepted. Subscriptions normally begin with the first of the four sourcebooks in the current publication year of the series. When ordering, please indicate if you prefer your subscription to begin with the first issue of the *coming* year.

Single copies are available at $7.95 when payment accompanies order, and *all single-copy orders under $25.00 must include payment* (California, New Jersey, New York, and Washington, D.C., residents please include appropriate sales tax.) For billed orders, cost per copy is $7.95 plus postage and handling. (Prices subject to change without notice.)

Bulk orders (ten or more copies) of any individual sourcebook are available at the following discounted prices: 10–49 copies, $7.15 each; 50–100 copies, $6.35 each; over 100 copies, *inquire.* Sales tax and postage and handling charges apply as for single copy orders.

To ensure correct and prompt delivery, all orders must give either the *name of an individual* or an *official purchase order number.* Please submit your order as follows:

Subscriptions: specify series and year subscription is to begin.
Single Copies: specify sourcebook code (such as, IR8) and first two words of title.

Mail orders for United States and Possessions, Latin America, Canada, Japan, Australia, and New Zealand to:
Jossey-Bass Inc., Publishers
433 California Street
San Francisco, California 94104

Mail orders for all other parts of the world to:
Jossey-Bass Limited
28 Banner Street
London EC1Y 8QE

New Directions for Institutional Research Series
Marvin W. Peterson, *Editor-in-Chief*
Patrick T. Terenzini, *Associate Editor*

Contents

The Association for Institutional Research was created in 1966 to benefit, assist, and advance research leading to improved understanding, planning, and operation of institutions of higher education. Publication policy is set by its Publications Board.

Editors' Notes

The United States and other developed nations are now in the midst of a transformation that may induce as much social change as the industrial revolution did. Central to this transformation, Masuda (1981) states, is the current "period of innovation in a new societal technology based on the combination of computer and communications technology, quite unlike any of the past. Its substance is information, which is invisible. This new societal technology will bring about societal transformation which . . is unprecedented." This transformation can be expected to induce fundamental changes in the economic, political, and institutional structures of society; corresponding impacts on higher education can also be expected, although their nature is uncertain. Profound, lifelong consequences of this transformation can be anticipated for most individuals. For example, what implications will these developments have for the kinds of skills, attitudes, and knowledge students need to acquire? For faculty members? For the allocation of resources to and within institutions? For relationships among industry, the military, and higher education? Will industrial or military demands for people competent in information technology exceed the ability of colleges and universities to produce them? What effects will increased capacities for storing, retrieving, and communicating information have on libraries, research, and institutional management? What repercussions will the new technologies have for providing educational services?

Parallel with the developments in telecommunications and computers, another social change has been occurring in our society. Not only is the number of eighteen-year-olds declining, but the society as a whole is aging. It is forecast that the over-sixty-five age group will grow from 10 percent to 14 percent of the total population by the year 2010—a dramatic increase of 40 percent. Indeed, by the year 2025, this age group may constitute nearly 20 percent of the population. Although projections like these are already producing debates—about the future of the Social Security System, for example— little attention has been given to their possible effects on higher education. Will an increasingly older population be willing to support low tuition? Does the role of higher education become more important to a society that must maintain or even increase productivity? Will retired but vital elderly persons return to school?

Much of our planning to date in higher education has focused on questions of internal effectiveness and efficiency, but given the period of rapid social change we have entered, it is imperative that we improve our abilities to assess changes in the external environment and examine their implications for

1

higher education. In this way, we will be able to develop better goals, strategies, and plans to take advantage of emerging opportunities and head off potentially damaging developments.

Futurists have developed numerous techniques for external environmental assessment and forecasting, but many of these are not well understood by institutional researchers, planners, or administrators. A recent volume in the New Directions for Institutional Research series focuses on using institutional research in strategic planning (Uhl, 1983). The chapters in that sourcebook, although they consider the problem of assessing the external environment (Glover and Holmes, 1983) and discuss the use of the Delphi technique in planning (Uhl, 1983), are primarily concerned with the contributions that traditional institutional research methods and perspectives make to institutional planning. The purpose of the present volume is to describe a variety of futures research techniques and to illustrate their utility for strategic planning in institutional research.

As our modern industrial society becomes increasingly specialized, we find ourselves increasingly challenged by new ideas and developments emerging outside our own fields of specialty. The history of forecasting traces a growing appreciation of the necessity of considering external developments, particularly unexpected events. In Chapter One, William L. Renfro and James L. Morrison review the organizational requirements for developing a capability to anticipate external developments. In Chapter Two, they focus on specific environmental scanning techniques, including sources and procedures for gathering scanning information. They also discuss the different kinds of scanning as well as the various procedures for organizing and maintaining a continuous, mature scanning function.

Peter Wagschall, in Chapter Three, describes a process that uses several judgmental techniques in combination to tap the unique and rich resources available to a scanning committee. Corporate scanners usually have to search for experts who are able to address issues that are well beyond the particular competence of their corporations. Colleges and universities often provide such experts. Wagschall's chapter describes a simple way in which colleges and universities can tap these resident experts for the institutions' own benefit. The judgmental methods used in this approach include the future wheel, a version of cross-impact analysis, and scenario-writing.

Chapter Four, by Richard Heydinger and Rene Zentner, explores scenario writing, a technique for integrating a variety of complex scanning results into a holistic, integrated view of a possible future. Heydinger and Zentner focus special attention on the use of multiple scenarios to describe a range of alternative futures.

Selwyn Enzer, in Chapter Five, concludes our presentation of futures research techniques per se with a review of the principal issues now being addressed in futures research, particularly the question of how it can be improved to enhance our present state-of-the-art forecasting methods, QUEST and INTERAX.

In Chapter Six, Heydinger considers the implications that the perspectives and techniques described in this sourcebook have for institutional research offices and for their relationship to institutional strategic planning. Chapter Seven, by Boucher, closes this volume with an annotated bibliography of salient literature describing the various futures research techniques that may be useful to institutional researchers.

James L. Morrison
William L. Renfro
Wayne I. Boucher
Editors

References

Glover, R. H., and Holmes, J. "Assessing the External Environment." In N. P. Uhl (Ed.), *Using Research for Strategic Planning.* New Directions for Institutional Research, no. 37. San Francisco. Jossey-Bass, 1983.

Masuda, Y. *The Information Society as Post-Industrial Society.* Tokyo, Japan: Institute for the Information Society, 1981.

Uhl, N. P. (Ed.). *Using Reserach for Strategic Planning.* New Directions for Institutional Research, no. 37. San Francisco: Jossey-Bass, 1983.

Uhl, N. P. "Using the Delphi Technique in Institutional Planning." In. N. P. Uhl (Ed.), *Using Research for Strategic Planning.* New Directions for Institutional Research, no. 37. San Francisco: Jossey-Bass, 1983.

James L. Morrison is professor of education at the University of North Carolina, Chapel Hill. He is on the board of directors of the Association for the Study of Higher Education and serves as chair of the Special Interest Group on Futures Research, American Educational Research Association.

William L. Renfro is president of Policy Analysis Company, Inc., 148 E Street, S.E., Washington, D.C. He is issues management editor of The Futurist *and serves on the board of directors of the Issues Management Association.*

Wayne I. Boucher is senior research associate at the Center for Futures Research of the Graduate School of Business Administration, University of Southern California. His books on forecasting, futures research, and strategic planning include The Study of the Future: An Agenda for Research *and* Systems Analysis and Policy Planning.

*Developing an environmental scanning system can identify
important emerging issues that may constitute either threats
or opportunities. This process helps institutions allocate their
resources in a way that anticipates and responds to changes in
the external environment.*

The Scanning Process:
Getting Started

William L. Renfro
James L. Morrison

During the past twenty years, forecasting for planning purposes has included more and more use of information about the environment external to institutions. In traditional forecasting and planning, an organization would focus on its own current performance as the basis for its outlook on the future, and early forecasting and planning techniques were developed to support this internal perspective, which assumed that changing conditions in the external world would not require re-evaluation of internal workings. Nowadays, however, this assumption has become increasingly unacceptable.

By the 1930s, the pace of changing external conditions led Alfred North Whitehead (1931) to observe, "The point is that in the past the time span of important change was considerably longer than that of a single human life. Thus mankind was trained to adapt itself to fixed conditions. But today this time span in considerably shorter than that of human life, and accordingly our training must prepare individuals to face a novelty of conditions. But there can be no preparation for the unknown (p. xix)."

Since the internal organizational perspective was premised on a much more stable society, economy, and overall environment than was to be the case in the 1960s and the 1970s, forecasters and planners were compelled to develop

J. L. Morrison, W. L. Renfro, and W. I. Boucher (Eds.). *Applying Methods and Techniques of Futures Research.*
New Directions for Institutional Research, no. 39. San Francisco: Jossey-Bass, September 1983.

methods and concepts to include more and more of the external world in internal forecasting. For example, conventional trend extrapolation was modified so that it could take account of the effects of unexpected events in the outside world. This new method became known as trend-impact analysis. Cross-impact analysis was developed to explore the interaction and interconnection of possible future events. Another method, systems modeling, was also modified to include external changes and became known as probabilistic system dynamics. The objective of these newer techniques was not to predict the future better—an increasingly elusive goal in a more turbulent world—but to provide better insight into the range of uncertainty facing managers.

Increased emphasis on potential changes in the external world continues today in issues management, an emerging field in which the inside-out perspective of traditional forecasting and planning is replaced by an outside-in perspective, so that external developments are given the prominence they warrant in the planning process. It is safe to assume that the allocation of significant resources to external environmental scanning will increase in importance as the pace of change continues or accelerates in the 1980s and beyond.

The Focus of Environmental Scanning

The precise origins of modern environmental scanning are unclear. (For an early approach, see Ogburn, 1933). Much of it originally focused on identifying economic developments. Soon, it came to include the tracking of prospective technological innovations, and then social trends and change. By the late 1970s, scanners recognized that they also needed to consider new legislative and regulatory requirements. Thus, at the simplest level, modern scanning now includes attention to economic developments, technological innovations, social change, and legislative and regulatory developments. These four areas are described below.

Economic Developments. As inflation and economic growth fluctuated in the 1960s, traditional planners began to see the importance of including explicit assumptions about alternative external economic environments in their internal plans. The shock of the mid-1970s energy crisis established the importance of considering a variety of possible external economic environments for all social institutions.

Technological Innovations. More and more industries have become aware of the need to understand the potential effects of new technologies on their functions, operations, and very existence. For example, the slide rule industry practically disappeared with the introduction of hand calculators. Nevertheless, though traditional technological lead times are growing shorter, it is still true that "if it isn't in the research labs today, it won't be on the market for five or ten years." This maxim allows us to maintain relative confidence in our ability to scan and forecast the emerging technological environment, a confidence which would be unjustified in economic or social forecasting.

Social Change. As individuals slowly adapt their personal behavior to changing environments, the new behavior patterns that gradually emerge tend to have radical implications for virtually every institution in the country. The life insurance industry, for example, found itself facing a crisis in the 1960s as more married women returned to or stayed in the labor force, providing second incomes and a new source of economic security for their families: Families with two incomes did not see the same need for life insurance protection that families with only one income perceived. Again, in higher education, social changes resulting from the civil rights movement, the antiwar movement, the women's movement, and increased student activism often forced colleges and universities to respond to such unfamiliar issues as student demands to participate on search committees, curriculum committees, boards of trustees, and so on. The Census Bureau and the Department of Labor also lost credibility as sources of population forecasts or labor force growth projections because they did not foresee a major social change: Many women delayed or indefinitely postponed their plans to have children, deciding instead to continue working. Throughout the 1960s and the 1970s, the Census Bureau's annual projections showed the birthrate increasing for the following year, but each new year of data showed it actually declining; only in the last year or so has the birthrate begun a slow upturn. For all practical purposes, the nuclear power industry has been suspended by social concern about the safety of nuclear power. The housing industry has experienced the effects of a shift away from large, suburban homes to city condominiums. Banks and other financial institutions have been forced to extend credit fairly to women, whether they are single, married, or divorced and whether they work in or outside the home.

None of the institutions facing these difficult social challenges in the 1960s and the 1970s could have anticipated them from internally focused perspectives. For example, life insurance became a better and better value throughout this period; other things being equal, life insurance sales probably would have soared as the baby boom population matured. The nuclear power industry stood ready in the 1970s to build the first assembly line for nuclear power plants, expecting that by the year 2000 almost a thousand plants would be scattered across the country. Clearly, our ability to forecast technological change does not extend to the social realm.

Legislative and Regulatory Developments. Increasingly, social issues have come to be expressed through new legislative and regulatory requirements. The automobile industry was unprepared for air pollution control and safety requirements, which seem only to aggravate its other new problem — fuel economy. Employers throughout the land have been faced with new requirements for occupational safety and health, pension reform, affirmative action, and age equity. The legislative and regulatory environment changed rapidly enough to make it difficult for businesses to plan new products and services. Colleges and universities have been charged with implementing the concept of equity through affirmative action and other requirements, and there have been major changes in facilities and in the demographic composition of student bodies and faculties.

Experience shows that the future and its changes almost always come with ample warning. Unfortunately, however, we often disregard, misinterpret, or fail to recognize the signals of change. In 1960 Rachel Carson wrote *Silent Spring*, launching the environment as an issue that has engulfed the automobile and electric power industries, as well as most of our heavy industries — ten years before the Environmental Protection Agency was created. President Eisenhower's Paley Commission warned the country in the early 1950s of an energy crisis in the mid-1970s. The civil rights movement and the current wave of the women's movement created activism in the 1960s, years before Congress expressed these movements' social goals in legislative and regulatory requirements.

The legislative and regulatory environment includes changes in political institutions, but is not particularly focused on changes in politics. (Republican presidents — Nixon and Ford — signed most of the recent social legislation, establishing, for example, the Environmental Protection Agency, the Occupational Safety and Health Administration, and the Employee Retirement Income Security Act.) The important element for scanning is legislative and regulatory policy, not the political affiliation of its implementers. Changes that affect legislative and regulatory policy, such as the shift in policy initiatives away from Congress to the states, are included in the legislative and regulatory category of scanning.

The Development Cycle of Issues

Many of the legal and regulatory changes that will be buffeting our institutions in the coming decades are in the earliest stages of development today. The development cycle of issues from changing social and personal values to final resolution is an open, known process. Issues which are addressed by the Congress on the national level progress through three main stages: (1) the public discussion/development stage; (2) the legislative stage in Congress; and (3) the regulatory stage in the authorized agency. The public stage often involves a defining event which provides focus for the issue (such as Love Canal, Three Mile Island, DC-10). While there is no set sequence for these early developments, most if not all issues evolve through these growth stages. The sequence in the Congress and in the regulatory stages is much more formalized and structured. The development cycle of public issues is summarized

Figure 1. The Development Cycle of Public Issues

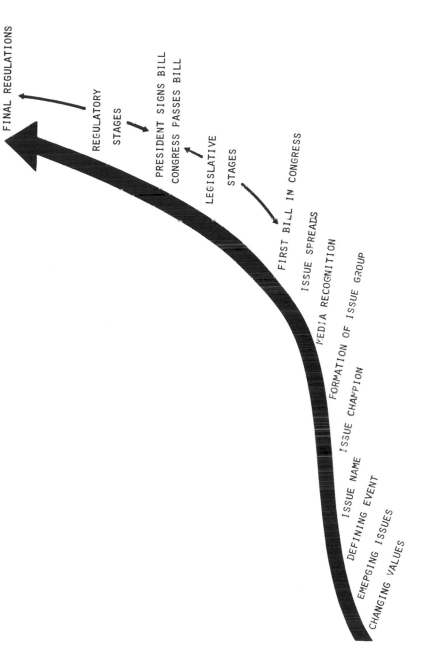

in Figure 1. The process of moving an issue from a wistful goal to a federal regulatory requirement is a process that takes years and sometimes decades. It took over fifty years, for example, for women's voting rights to be recognized. The labor movement spent more than thirty years to achieve recognition of its right to organize. Similar issues, which will be challenging our institutions of higher learning in the future, are in the early stages of development today— carcinogens in residence halls and classrooms, sunshine laws on university decision making, and institutional and personal liability for quality of teaching, among others. The signals of emerging issues are all around us.

How is it, then, that we do such a poor job of identifying these changes? The problems here are twofold. First, we tend to spend our time on issues that seem most important now. Important issues tend to be defined as those of the greatest immediacy; thus, even when we are aware of emerging issues, we do not have the time or the motivation to address them. Second, we may not be farsighted or comprehensive enough to see the emerging issues.

These two problems are compounded by the difficulty of coping with our modern print and telecommunications society. Managing the flood of information it makes possible is a major problem, and a skill required of all successful administrators. Nevertheless, it sometimes seems almost beyond our capacity to separate meaningful signals from the tremendous amount of noise that assaults us daily. A related difficulty is not seeing what we do not want to see: We ingest from our information resources those bits and pieces that tend to confirm positions and ideas we already have, screening out information that would force us to rethink our preconceived ideas, opinions, and attitudes. The scanning process is a conscious struggle against this selective blindness.

However difficult it is to identify what will be the issues of the future, or at least clarify the spectrum of possibilities, existing organizational resources and personnel are still key starting points for developing an environmental scanning function. While this function can be supported by external experts and specialists, most successful scanning programs have grown directly from the rich resources of talent and skills within institutions. Developing the scanning function from these resources is outlined in the following section.

Developing the Environmental Scanning Function

As with any new process introduced in an organization, there are two main barriers: mastering the new process and achieving the necessary organizational acceptance and commitment to make the process work well. These two barriers pose the following questions: How does the environmental scanning process work within an organization? What resources and personnel are needed? How do we develop the environmental scanning function within an existing organization? While the specific structure of the scanning function will vary according to the management style of a given institution, the purposes of the scanning function are the same for all institutions. The scanning structure described below is based on the experiences of major corporations and trade and professional associations. Their experiences may also be applied to institutions of higher education. The specific structure described below, of course, must be adapted for particular colleges or universities.

Using Inside Resources

Environmental scanning begins with gathering information about the external environment. This information comes from two distinct sources, one inside the organization and the other outside. For example, key administrators and faculty members could be asked, perhaps through an interview Delphi process, to identify the issues they believe will affect the institution in the future, and which are not now receiving the attention they will merit eventually. Such requests usually release a flood of responses, which shows that many important new developments facing the organization have already been anticipated by some key leaders, though the press of current emergencies and crisis management has given them little opportunity to reveal their longer-term concerns.

Administrators and selected faculty members could also be requested to describe where they find information about potential changes in the external world — the newspapers, magazines, trade publications, association journals, and other print or electronic media sources they regularly use. Typically, these surveys show that administrators all read basically the same publications — usually one or more local newspapers (but only selected sections), occasionally national newspapers (but, again, only selected sections) and the same magazines (*Time, Newsweek, U.S. News & World Report*, and so on). Institutional researchers probably read some of the same professional publications — *Research in Higher Education, Journal of Higher Education, The Chronicle of Higher Education, AAUP Bulletin, Higher Education Daily, Change*, and *New Directions for Institutional Research* — but also probably vary with respect to reading publications in their particular subject areas (for example, psychology, sociology, economics, and higher education). And, of course, faculty members in academic departments, as well as staff members in various administrative areas (housing, financial aid, and so on), probably read their own specialized publications.

The results of such surveys will most likely indicate that individuals within an organization already know much of what the organization as a whole needs to know, even though they are operating with self-imposed blinders. While organizing an environmental scanning function will not eliminate leaders' responsibility to consider the outside environment, scanning will ensure that external issues are included as a part of institutional management and decision making.

Using Outside Resources

Once the scanning committee (described below) is operating, question-naires may be distributed to panels of experts outside the institution. These experts could be selected and organized in terms of the four major scanning categories already discussed. External resources, such as an electronic-mail consortium in which information could be shared, can help the committee keep informed of issues identified by other institutions. A modest investment in newsletters, subscriptions to scanning resources, conferences, and even-tually original research will pay large dividends, too.

The Scanning Committee

Developing the scanning function within an organization is a most delicate matter. It must be an evolutionary process, since sudden organiza-tional change is disruptive and costly. While there are many ways the scan-ning function can be organized, by far the most popular is by means of a high-level, interdisciplinary committee. If scanning is assigned to a particular department or contracted out, the results can easily be ignored. Furthermore, cross-cutting impacts — for example, the impact of a technological develop-ment (the home computer) on social issues (the family) — will most likely be missed. For the widest appreciation of how emerging issues may interact, the scanning function must be interdisciplinary. Communication of scanning results to the whole institution is easiest on the basis of direct work with the institution's various leaders, rather than with their representatives. The scan-ning committee should be appointed by and accountable to the chief executive officer of the institution, and the chair of the committee should be one of his or her most trusted advisers.

Membership Selection

The first essential task related to the committee is selection of its mem-bers. There are no clear guidelines on exactly who should be involved; such judgments vary from organization to organization. Experience shows that a good balance between efficiency and completeness is reached when, ideally, the number of members attending a committee meeting does not exceed twelve to fifteen; in practice a number closer to ten is often optimal. Since there will always be some absentees, invitations to committee membership should perhaps be extended to the twelve to fourteen institutional leaders who have responsibilities in what will be the committee's various areas of concern. These leaders normally will include department heads, vice-presidents, deans, the provost, faculty members, trustees, and others. The institutional research office certainly should be represented, if not by the director, then by a senior assistant. (In all likelihood, the institutional research office would be responsible for the committee's staff support, and the director or assistant director would coordinate it.) Membership selection should ensure that all important stakeholders in positions of responsibility are either represented or actually members of the committee. A special effort also should be made to include the future leaders of the institution — those who will have to deal firsthand with issues now only beginning to emerge.

There are several reasons for high-level administrators to participate in scanning. First, their experience and broad overview of current operations, as well as their knowledge of reasonable future directions of the institution, are indispensible to informed evaluations of items identified by scanning. Second, using these individuals lessens problems of communication, recognition, and acceptance of change. As noted earlier, if scanning is delegated to a group of experts, whether inside or outside the university, the results may be ignored. Third, using top people helps develop in them a personal stake in the success of the scanning system, since each participant tends to relate everything he reads or hears to the question "What possible relevance does this have for the scanning committee and for my institution?" Indeed, this subtle outcome — the development of an active orientation to the external environment and to the future — may well be an outcome as important as any other.

There are several other advantages to using administrators. The time lag between the recognition of a new issue and its presentation to the institutional leadership is reduced, if not eliminated. When an issue arises that requires immediate action, the scanning committee is already in a position to serve the institutional leadership by offering experience and knowledge of relevant issues dealt with earlier within the institution or by others.

It should be emphasized that the scanning committee neither needs nor often has any specific or general authorization to take action on any of the issues it addresses; it serves as an advisory board to the president. In this sense, it works like the institutional planning office, preparing information to support the work of the authorized leaders. Of course, the scanning committee is available to the president, to be used as one of the resources of the university. The purpose of the scanning committee is to identify potentially important emerging issues, which may constitute either threats or opportunities. Once this task has been performed, the institution can allocate its resources in an orderly way to anticipate and respond to the changing external environment. The committee's function is necessarily advisory and its focus is long-term.

Committee Meetings

After the committee is organized and established, it can meet quarterly, usually for most of a day, at a site where interruptions are minimal. In the early stages, however, members may want to meet more often—perhaps monthly for the first year and bimonthly for the second year—before moving to a quarterly schedule. These decisions will depend on the development of the necessary staff (usually a single person) and on how well members accomplish the committee's necessary day-to-day tasks.

Issue Definitions

In its monthly or quarterly meetings, the committee will consider and discuss issues gathered from internal and external resources. The staff prepares a definition and a background statement for each issue. On request, the staff also provides other background research materials that are readily available from other resources at little or no cost. The chair of the committee conducts meetings and various exercises, often accomplishing this task initially in conjunction with an outside professional facilitator. Once the chair is experienced in this process, the outside facilitator usually moves into a support role.

Assessing Impacts: An Example

In discussing the various issues presented to the committee and their potential implications, the facilitator can guide the committee through the exercise known as the impact wheel. The impact wheel is a structured process designed to address the wide range of a new development's possible consequences. Every member of the committee nominates a possible impact or a consequence of a given development. After all the first-order impacts have been collected, the process is repeated. Each first-order impact is treated as though it were a new given development, and the task is to identify its particular impacts, which in turn become second-order impacts for the original given development. The process can be repeated for second-, third-, and fourth-order impacts. Third-order impacts often are sufficient to highlight most of a particular development's potential consequences. (See Chapter 3 of this sourcebook for a detailed discussion of impact wheels.)

Issue Evaluation

Following discussion of all the issues, the committee can establish the priority of the issues for detailed evaluation or even action. One method for accomplishing this process is to use a probability impact chart. In this process, two similar but separate evaluations are made for each issue. First, the group is asked to estimate the probability that the issue might materialize fully within the planning period (e.g., the next five years). Next, the probable impact of this issue on the institution is assessed, assuming that the issue has fully materialized. The chair then tabulates the results for each issue by copying all the individual votes onto a single chart that shows how all the committee members voted on each issue. To ensure the freedom to express controversial, unpopular, or threatening opinions, voting must be anonymous. Sample results of a tabulated probability impact chart are shown in Figure 2. Two events are evaluated on this chart; the votes on the first are indicated by zeros and the votes on the second by Xs. As can be seen, the group judged the 0 event to have low probability, but was quite divided on its potential impact. On the X event, the group is in close agreement on both probability (high) and impact (high).

Interpretation of results like those in Figure 2 depends on the purpose to be served. If, for example, the purpose is to alert administrators to possible surprising developments disclosed by the scanning process, then items like event X are ranked well above items like event 0, assuming that no one had previously expected event X to happen. If, however, the purpose is to identify items that appear to warrant additional study, then event 0 will rank much higher than event X. If the objective is to eliminate items from further consideration, then all of the developments can be ranked on the basis of their perceived probability and impact, and those scoring lowest on both factors can be dropped.

Guidance like this can usually be obtained simply by inspecting and discussing the voting pattern on the chart; no computations are necessary. When the set of issues is very large, however, a more formal treatment may be necessary, in which, for example, averages of the votes on probability and impact are derived and these values are used, singly or in combination, for the various screening tasks. (The "weighted importance" shown in Figure 2 is the product of these two averages. It can be used for some of these purposes.) Of course, when the votes are obviously scattered—for example, some members think the issue's impact is positive, some think it is negative, and others think it is nonexistent—additional discussion and anonymous voting may be required before any sorting of the set can be accomplished. It will often turn out that such issues need to be redefined as subissues or in terms of their importance to particular components of the university. For example, members concerned about federal aid requirements may see these requirements as an issue of high importance; other members who are not knowledgeable or concerned about federal aid requirements may see them as less important, particularly as compared to their own pet issues. When issues produce such polar

Figure 2. Probability Impact Chart Summarizing Seven Votes For Two Different Events

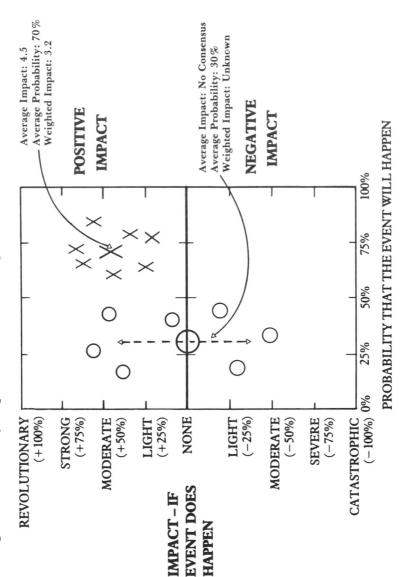

Average Impact: 4.5
Average Probability: 70%
Weighted Impact: 3.2

POSITIVE IMPACT

Average Impact: No Consensus
Average Probability: 30%
Weighted Impact: Unknown

NEGATIVE IMPACT

REVOLUTIONARY (+100%)

STRONG (+75%)

MODERATE (+50%)

LIGHT (+25%)

NONE

LIGHT (−25%)

MODERATE (−50%)

SEVERE (−75%)

CATASTROPHIC (−100%)

IMPACT – IF EVENT DOES HAPPEN

0%   25%   50%   75%   100%

PROBABILITY THAT THE EVENT WILL HAPPEN

Note: Xs show consensus about a very probable event with high, positive impact.
0s show an event with consensus on probability (low), but not on impact.

responses, the issues must be rephrased or else the question of its importance must be redefined. Such issues must never be deleted from the process, however. In fact, polarizing issues may already have stymied institutional decision making and so need prompt attention. Also, at least for some members, these issues often have the greatest potential for surprise.

Strategy Selection

Once issue priority has been set according to weighted importance, the committee is ready to consider appropriate responses to each issue, and for each one the committee has four basic choices. One option is to recommend immediate action to the president. Support for the committee's strategy recommendation is assigned to an issue action task force made up partly of committee members and partly of other available persons. For example, if an issue concerned a human resources question, then the vice-president for administration might lead the task force. The second choice is to form an issue strategy task force similar to the issue action task force. This option is used when it is obvious that some action is needed, but it is not clear what it should be. This task force's assignment is to identify the possibilities. The third option is to form an issue research task force. It investigates the issue, developing additional information, background, and potential options and strategies, and reports back to the scanning committee at its next regular meeting. The fourth choice, for issues of lesser importance, is for the scanning committee to assign itself continued special scanning of the issue for any relevant new developments. As a practical matter, the scanning committee should assign itself and its task force members no more than four to six issues at any time. (With all its resources, even Connecticut General, a part of the CIGNA Corporation, limits itself to just seven active issues each year.) In the case of continued special scanning, the committee chair should assign only one issue to each committee member, as a practical limit to the number of such issues. An available staff person can be made responsible for additional special scanning.

The final item on the agenda for the committee at each meeting should be a roundtable discussion of how the scanning process is working, what needs to be added to the scanning literature, whether additional questionnaires should be administered inside or outside the university, and how the program is going, in general. The stages of the scanning process, as described above, are shown in Figure 3.

Summary

Scanning the external environment will become more and more essential to colleges and universities in the coming decade. This institutional plan-

Figure 3. Organization of Environmental Scanning Function

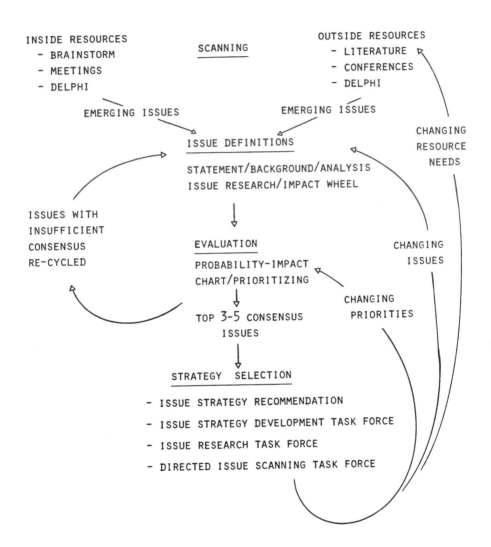

INSIDE RESOURCES
- BRAINSTORM
- MEETINGS
- DELPHI

SCANNING

OUTSIDE RESOURCES
- LITERATURE
- CONFERENCES
- DELPHI

EMERGING ISSUES

EMERGING ISSUES

CHANGING
RESOURCE
NEEDS

ISSUE DEFINITIONS

STATEMENT/BACKGROUND/ANALYSIS
ISSUE RESEARCH/IMPACT WHEEL

ISSUES WITH
INSUFFICIENT
CONSENSUS
RE-CYCLED

EVALUATION

PROBABILITY-IMPACT
CHART/PRIORITIZING

CHANGING
ISSUES

TOP 3-5 CONSENSUS
ISSUES

CHANGING
PRIORITIES

STRATEGY SELECTION

- ISSUE STRATEGY RECOMMENDATION
- ISSUE STRATEGY DEVELOPMENT TASK FORCE
- ISSUE RESEARCH TASK FORCE
- DIRECTED ISSUE SCANNING TASK FORCE

ning technique provides the maximum lead time for adapting to emerging issues that may entail positive or adverse effects for an institution. This chapter has described, in very general terms, the organizational features of a mature scanning process. Each institution will need to derive its own scanning structure. Obviously, the role of the institutional research office is crucial in determining whatever structure is to be established, for it is most likely that this office will be providing staff support. Of course, the public affairs office may also provide valuable support, since employees of these offices frequently perform scanning functions, although usually only with respect to articles focusing on the particular institution, but this focus could be broadened.

Few if any institutions have established scanning functions to the extent described in this chapter. Developing scanning committees requires time, energy, and money that few institutional research offices currently have. One way an organization can reduce these expenditures is to establish a consortium of institutional research offices linked through electronic mail to share the scanning task. Small institutions in particular may want to involve faculty members more actively.

One question not specifically addressed in this chapter concerns the relationship between the scanning committee, as outlined here, and the chancellor's or president's advisory committee. The scanning committee's task could be to identify issues the scan has revealed as having a probable impact on the organization, while the presidential advisory committee could establish strategy committees to handle these issues. Specific institutions would resolve this question individually.

A final comment: The scanning process must be as open as possible; any member of the institution should be able to nominate issues. Scanning committee meetings should be open to authorized observers. The scanning function will fail if administrators come to believe that the scanning committee or its task forces are assuming responsibilities assigned to others, without consultation. There is probably no greater threat to the scanning process than the growth of this belief, whether or not it is based in fact.

References and Sources

Aguilar, F. J. *Scanning the Business Environment.* New York: Macmillan, 1967.

Boe, A. R. "Fitting the Corporation to the Future." *Public Relations Quarterly,* 1979, *24* (1), 4-6.

Edrich, H. "Keeping a Weather Eye on the Future." *Planning Review,* 1980, *8* (1), 11-14.

Ewing, R. P. "The Uses of Futurist Techniques in Issues Management." *Public Relations Quarterly,* 1979, *24* (4), 15-19.

Godiwalla, Y. "Environmental Scanning—Does It Help the Chief Executive?" *Long Range Planning,* 1980, *13* (5), 87-99.

Hegarty, W. H. "Strategic Planning in the 1980s — Coping with Complex External Forces." *Planning Review,* 1981, *9* (5), 8–12.

Kast, F. "Scanning the Future Environment: Social Indicators." *California Management Review,* 1980, *23* (1), 22–32.

Klein, H. E., and Newman, W. H. "How to Integrate New Environmental Forces into Strategic Planning." *Management Review,* 1980, *69* (7), 40–48.

Nadelson, C. "Emerging Issues for College Students in the 1980s." *Journal of American College Health,* 1983, *31,* 177–184.

Ogburn, W. F. *Recent Social Trends in the United States.* New York: McGraw-Hill, 1933.

Preble, J. F. "Corporate Use of Environmental Scanning." *University of Michigan Business Review,* 1978, *30* (5), 12–17.

Renfro, W. L. "Congress, Corporations, and Crystal Balls: A Partnership for the Future?" *Planning Review,* 1980, *8* (4), 36–42.

Renfro, W. L. "Managing the Issues of the 1980s." *The Futurist,* 1982, *16* (4), 61–66.

Renfro, W. L., and Morrison, J. L. "Merging Two Futures Concepts: Application to Educational Policy." *The Futurist,* 1982, *16* (5), 54–56.

Terry, P. T. "Mechanisms for Environmental Scanning." *Long Range Planning,* 1977, *10* (3), 2–9.

Weiner, E. "Future Scanning for Trade Groups and Companies." *Harvard Business Review,* 1976, *54* (5), 14, 174–175.

Whitehead, A. N. "On Foresight." In W. B. Donham (Ed.), *Business Adrift.* New York: McGraw-Hill, 1931.

Vanderwicken, P. "'Externalysis': A New Dimension in Planning." *Planning Review,* 1982, *10* (4), 24–27.

William L. Renfro is president of Policy Analysis Company, Inc., 148 E Street, S.E., Washington, D.C. 20003. He is issues management editor of The Futurist *and serves on the board of directors of the Issues Management Association.*

James L. Morrison is professor of education at the University of North Carolina, Chapel Hill. He is on the board of directors of the Association for the Study of Higher Education and serves as chair of the Special Interest Group on Futures Research, American Educational Research Association.

Scanning requires knowing how to scan and what to scan.

The Scanning Process: Methods and Uses

William L. Renfro
James L. Morrison

The future is simply everything that might happen, including everything that will happen. The process of scanning, tracking, and maintaining some state of awareness of everything is obviously both impossible and unnecessary. This chapter focuses on developing a rational scanning process that reaches a balance between what is needed and what is possible within the limitations of an institution's resources. It begins with a discussion of the different kinds of scanning, which kind to use at each stage of the process, and why. The importance of and rationale for involving committee members in the scanning process is reviewed in the context of the organizational and communication issues surrounding the development of scanning taxonomies. The issue of how to bound the scanning process is addressed—first, in general terms of the "interesting future"; second, in specific terms of selecting the subjects and kinds of resources to scan. Finally, the necessary support functions of the scanning committee are discussed, along with the utility of tapping existing university resources to support the work of the committee.

J. L. Morrison, W. L. Renfro, and W. I. Boucher (Eds.). *Applying Methods and Techniques of Futures Research.*
New Directions for Institutional Research, no. 39. San Francisco: Jossey-Bass, September 1983.

Passive, Active, and Directed Scanning

Scanning includes a broad range of personal and organizational activities. As it is defined here, the basic element of scanning is a process of screening a large body of information for some particular bit or bits of information. This information is identified by specifying screening criteria. For example, some people scan newspaper headlines for particular kinds of articles (for example, only those containing historical information). Others scan for articles containing shock, horror, or disaster. When information meeting the criteria is found in a newspaper, scanning stops, and the article is read. Once the article is read, scanning resumes. A similar process is followed when people scan magazines at a newsstand. Scanning, therefore, consists of searching an information resource, consciously or not, for a particular kind of information, which is then subjected to special attention.

This process has four specific aspects: (1) selecting information resources to scan, (2) searching or screening for information resources, (3) identifying criteria by which to scan, and (4) determining special action for the scanning results. Specification of each aspect determines the kind of scanning—passive, active, and directed. (For an excellent, detailed discussion of scanning used by business executives, see Aguilar, 1967, pp. 9–30.)

Passive Scanning. Every person is involved in scanning at some level of effort almost continuously. Whatever a particular individual's interests, goals, personal values, or professional objectives, it is an element of human nature to respond to incoming important information. This continous scanning at an almost unconscious level is called *passive scanning*. No effort is made to select a particular information resource to scan; the scanning criteria are obscure, unspecified, and often continually changing. Only ad hoc decisions are made on the results of this type of scanning. This passive scanning has traditionally been a major source of information about the external world for most decision makers and, hence, for their organizations.

It is clear that people direct special attention to areas of known or historical importance, areas that have provided either threats or opportunities in the past. For example, people concerned about their professional development do more than passive scanning of available resources for specific kinds of information desired. This is not an unconscious activity, but rather an active, self-imposed responsibility. It is clearly distinguished from passive scanning, it is active scanning.

The external environment historically has been a subject of at least some interest to most people, and it requires at least passive scanning at some level for maintenance of a person's chosen level of fluency in current or emerging issues. Changes in the external environment have moved such scanning from an element of good citizenship to a professional requirement, from a low-level personal-interest activity to a high-level professional responsibility requiring active scanning—more like the special scanning used for subjects of particular importance, such as career development.

Active Scanning. The four components of active scanning are different from those of passive scanning. For example, the search or screening process is at a much higher level of attention. The information resources being scanned are specifically selected for their known or expected richness in the desired information. These resources may include some but usually not all of the regular incoming resources of passive scanning; thus, a member of a scanning committee would not actively scan hobby literature on sailing for emerging issues of potential importance to the university. This is not to say that such issues will not appear in this literature, but that passive scanning should be sufficient to pick up any that do.

In active scanning, the screening criteria are very clearly specified. Scanning for emerging issues, trends, and future events that may signal changes in the external environment requires broad criteria to assure completeness of the scanning. These criteria usually focus on questions like these: Does this item have present or potential relevance to current or planned operations of the institution? Is the combination of the likelihood and the impact of the item sufficient to justify notifying the scanning committee? A shift in polar ice caps could have tremendous impact but be just too unlikely in the foreseeable future to warrant inclusion in the scanning process. It is not part of the current "interesting future."

The interesting future is a very small part of the whole future. This part of the future is bounded by the human dimensions of time, knowledge, and resources. The interesting future comprises only that range of alternative outcomes for which it is practical to plan or take action now or within a foreseeable period. For almost all issues, the interesting future falls within the next fifty to seventy-five years at the outside, although most issues will actually fall within the one- to ten-year range. This time frame is defined as the period in which timely and practical major policy options would begin to have significant impact, if planned or adopted now.

The issues-policy-response time frame depends on the cycle time of the issue. For Social Security financing, the interesting future certainly runs from now to at least the next seventy-five years—the life expectancy of children born now. For financial issues, the interesting future may be the next several budget cycles—just two or three years. For a new federal regulatory requirement that may be imposed next year, the interesting future runs from now until then.

The interesting future is bounded by a measure of the uncertainty of an issue's actually developing. Developments that are all but certain either to happen or not to happen are of little interest in scanning: As institutions have little ability to affect these happenings, they should be referred to appropriate departments for inclusion in planning functions. The aging of the "baby boom," for example, is certain to happen and should be factored into current strategy-planning processes. Potential new impacts of this development, such as growing competition among medical care providers for federal resources, should be forwarded to scanning committees for evaluation of probability and importance. Thus, the interesting future is composed of developments that are uncertain, important if they do or do not happen, and responsive to current policy options. These are the general criteria for items that members of scanning committees should be including in their work.

Finally, the special treatment of the results of active scanning is known (or at least planned) in advance. This special treatment may be any action treating an item that satisfies the scanning criteria in a way distinct from how other items are treated. In the example of passive scanning of newspaper headlines, the special treatment was reading the article. In an organizational scanning system, the special treatment is usually reporting the item to the scanning committee.

A second dimension of scanning concerns the time element of the information resources being scanned. Information resources are either already existing resources, such as library archives, or continuing resources, defined as resources that continue to come in over time, such as a magazine's arriving by subscription. Passive scanning uses all incoming resources—conversations at home, over lunch, at the office, on TV or radio, at conferences and at meetings; memos; notes; or any other source of incoming information. Passive scanning rarely involves existing resources. Active scanning involves the conscious selection of continuing resources, which from time to time may be supplemented by existing resources, as needed. For example, an item that results from scanning continuing resources may require directed scanning of an existing resource for development of the necessary background, context, or history to determine an appropriate response.

Directed Scanning. The active scanning of a selected existing resource for specific, known items is directed scanning. Usually this scanning continues until the items are located, not necessarily until the resources are exhausted. For example, if a member of the scanning committee knows that a needed article was in a particular journal at some time last year, an assistant can be directed to scan the tables of contents of all volumes of the journal until the article is located. Since the specific desired item is known and the resource can be specified, the scanning committee can delegate whatever directed scanning is necessary.

Scanning for the Committee. To anticipate the changing conditions of its external environment, the institution needs both active and passive scanning of general and selected continuing information resources. While the committee will also need occasional directed scanning of existing resources, members are involved only in scanning their personal, current, and selected continuing resources. The specific criteria of scanning are developed along the dimensions discussed above. The results of this process will be reported to the scanning committee for evaluation. This may be a simple task of clipping or copying an article and sending or bringing it to the committee. The chair of the committee (or its staff, if any) compiles incoming clippings as preparation for the discussion of new issues at the next regular meeting. In this task, the chair will look for reinforcing signals; for coincident items, each of which may only have sufficient importance if both happen; for items that may call for active or directed scans of new or different resources; and for information about the interesting future.

Developing Scanning Taxonomies

Any number of taxonomies, lists, and mechanisms have been used to organize, structure, and bound the scanning process. All of these taxonomies attempt to satisfy several conflicting objectives. First, the taxonomy must be complete, in that every possible item resulting from the scanning has a logical place to be classified. Second, every such item should have only one place in the filing system. Third, the system must have few enough categories to be readily usable, but at the same time must be detailed enough to separate different issues.

An early task for the scanning committee and its staff is to develop a specialized taxonomy focused on the issues of greatest concern to the institution. The committee can use any method it chooses to select these categories. Whatever method is used, it should be rigorous, objective, thorough, democratic, and—to the extent possible—anonymous. One way to meet these criteria is to use a questionnaire based on an existing issues taxonomy. The U.S. Congress organizes its pending legislation into nearly 200 categories. This list, shown in Figure 1, can be used as a questionnaire, with respondents being asked to rate the relative importance of each category and expand categories that may have particular importance to the institution. For example, under the category of higher education, the committee may want to add subcategories concerning issues of tenure and the academic marketplace. Alternatively, the committee may want to develop its taxonomy under the categories of social, technical, economic, or legislative and regulatory change. The advantage of using a detailed taxonomy is the assurance of thoroughness and completeness, even if only 10 to 15 percent of the categories are adopted. The advantage of starting with these four categories is simplicity.

Figure 1. Classification Categories Used by the U.S. Congress for Pending Legislation

Accounting and auditing	Elementary and secondary education	Judiciary	Practical politics
Aeronautics	Environment	Juvenile delinquency	Presidents [U.S.]
Aerospace industries	Environmental economics	Labor	Press
Africa	Environmental health	Land use	Prisons
Agriculture	Environmental law	Latin America	Procurement
Air pollution	Equal employment opportunity	Law	Psychology
Alcoholism	Executive departments	Local finance	Public administration
Anti-poverty program	Executive reorganization	Local taxation	Public finance
Antitrust law	Families	Manpower training programs	Public health
Arms control	Federal advisory bodies	Marine transportation	Public lands
Asia	Federal aid to education	Materials management	Public opinion polls
Astronautics	Fisheries	Medicaid	Public welfare
Astronomy	Food	Medical economics	Regional development
Atomic energy	Food relief	Medical personnel	Religion
Birth control	Foreign economic relations	Medicare	Research and development
Blacks	Foreign economics	Medicine	Right of privacy
Business and society	Foreign relations	Mental health	Science manpower
Campaign funds	Forests and forestry	Middle East	Science policy
Canada	Future	Military assistance	Small business
Census	Government employees	Military justice	Social sciences
Chemicals	Government information	Military personnel	Social security
Child welfare	Guaranteed annual income	Mines and mineral resources	Solid wastes
Civil liberties	Handicapped	Minorities	Standards
Coastal areas	Health facilities	Money and banking	State governments
Communism	Health insurance	National defense	Systems analysis
Computers	Higher education	National priorities	Taxation
Congress	Highways	National disasters	Technology and civilization
Congressional districts	History [U.S.]	National resources	Technology assessment
Constitution [U.S.]	Housing	Noise	Telecommunication
Consumer protection	Housing finance	Occupational health and safety	Territories
Corporations	Immigration	Oceanography	Transportation
Credit	Indians	Old age	Urban areas
Crimes and offenses	Industrial organization	Outdoor recreation	Urban development
Criminal procedure	Industrial technology	Pacific area	Veterans
Defense economics	Insurance	Parks	Violence
Developing countries	Intelligence activities	Patents and inventions	Vocational education
District of Columbia	Intergovernmental fiscal relations	Pensions	War and peace
Drug abuse	Intergovernmental relations	Pesticides	Water Pollution
Drugs	Internal security	Polar regions	Water resources development
Earth sciences	International agencies	Police	Waterways
Eastern Europe	International corporations	Political ethics	Western Europe
Economic conditions	International economic relations	Political science	Wildlife conservation
Economic policy	International environmental affairs	Population	Women
Education	International finance	Pornography	Workers' compensation
Election law	International law	Postal service	Youth in politics
Electoral college	International relations	Poverty	
Electronics	International science affairs	Power resources	

When the questionnaire is complete, the top categories should be selected for scanning. The number here will be determined by the size of the committee—a ten- to twelve-member committee can handle no more than twenty-five to forty assigned categories for scanning, with each member having responsibility for two to three categories and the relevant sources to scan for each of these categories. The list of categories then becomes the subject index of the scanning files.

With this list and the publications and other resources already being scanned, the committee can identify the categories for which assigned scanning is necessary. Here, the kind of resource used takes on importance. For example, alcoholism may be an issue selected for scanning, but for which no current resource can be identified. For this issue, generic and secondary resources may be sufficient—newspapers, national weekly magazines, or other resources in the passive scanning network. Nevertheless, the resources designated for this issue should be identified along with their designated scanners. Of course, a particular publication or resource may cover more than a single category, and it may take several publications to cover a single issue adequately.

What to Scan

Determining which materials to scan is an extremely important but difficult task. It is obviously better to err on the side of inclusion at this point, but there is a clear limit to how much material committee members can scan. The decisions made here will largely determine the kind, content, and volume of information presented to the scanning committee and will ultimately determine the information's value to the institution. Obviously, this question deserves substantial initial and continuing attention.

All scanning committee members should increase their consciousness of their own passive scanning. In the flow of each person's continuing resources, the special screen of the scanning criteria should be added. This is a level of sensitivity that has to be learned with experience. It must be a rule of the committee that information in any form is acceptable. The process of passing notes, clippings, or copies from any resource must become second nature. The scanning coordinator or staff person will have the responsibility of processing the incoming flow for formal review by the committee.

The committee must also address the question of the resources it will actively scan. There are several aspects of available resources to consider in making this decision. First, as already noted, a survey of the committee will show the specific resources now included in its passive scanning. A list of these resources should be prepared. Next, the committee must consider the kinds of resources it should be scanning. This step involves thinking about content and kinds of resources—generic to all issues, only special issues, emerging or first impression of issues, the spread of issues, and so on.

In the process of assigning resources to issues, the committee should also consider the media mix it is using. The dimensions of media range from periodic books to annual or periodical publications, from print to electronic resources. The news media, for example, can play a major role in spreading an issue to new groups, defining an issue, and sometimes creating a national issue from a local one. (For the publications component of a scanning program, a fairly complete list of journals and newsletters focusing on the general field of higher education or specific aspects of the field is shown in Figures 2 and 3, respectively.) With respect to publications focusing on external issues, the committee may want to review those used by the American Council of Life Insurance in its Trends Analysis Program. (This list of over 100 periodicals is shown in Figure 4.) Other resources used in scanning are discussed below.

Popular Scanning Resources

Newspapers constitute a major scanning resource. Indeed, a balance of national newspapers should be scanned on a continuing basis. As each national newspaper has its particular focuses and biases, four to six national newspapers should be covered by the members of the committee. Usually, these

Figure 2. Journals Focusing on the Field of Higher Education

AAHE Bulletin
Academe
AGB Reports
Alternative Higher Education: The Journal of Nontraditional Studies
American Journal of Pharmaceutical Education
American Scholar
Assessment in Higher Education
Australian Journal of Education
Canadian Journal of Higher Education
CASE Currents
CAUSE/EFFECT
Change
College and University
College Board Review
College Store Journal
Education Policy Bulletin
Educational Record
European Journal of Education
Graduate Woman
Higher Education
Higher Education Review
Improving College and University Teaching
International Journal of Institutional Management in Higher Education
Journal of Architectural Education
Journal of College and University Law
Journal of Dental Education
Journal of Education for Social Work
Journal of Higher Education
Journal of Legal Education
Journal of Medical Education
Journal of Optometric Education
Journal of Podiatric Education
Journal of Student Financial Aid
Journal of Tertiary Education and Administration
Journal of the College and University Personnel Association
Journal of the Society of Research Administrators
Journal of Veterinary Medical Education
Liberal Education
NACADA Journal
National Forum: Phi Kappa Phi Journal
New Directions for Experiential Learning
New Directions for Higher Education
New Directions for Institutional Advancement
New Directions for Institutional Research
New Universities Quarterly
Planning for Higher Education
Research in Higher Education
The Review of Higher Education
Studies in Higher Education
Teaching at a Distance
University Administration
Vestes

Note: This list of journals is modified from one used by the ERIC Clearinghouse for Higher
Education in their indexing and abstracting of articles for the monthly bibliographic
journal, *Current Index of Journals in Education.*

Figure 3. Newsletters Focusing on the Field of Higher Education

AAC Update (Association of American Colleges)
AACJC Letter (American Association of Community and Junior Colleges)
AAHE Bulletin (American Association for Higher Education)
AALS News (Association of American Law Schools)
Academe (American Association of University Professors
Accreditation (Council on Postsecondary Accreditation)
ACCU Update (Association of Catholic Colleges and Universities)
ACER Newsletter (Australian Council for Educational Research Ltd.)
ACSA News (Association of Collegiate Schools of Architecture)
Action Update (Action Committee for Higher Education)
Agency for Instructional T.V. Newsletter
A.C.U. Bulletin (Association of Commonwealth Universities)
AGB Notes (Association of Governing Boards)
AGHE Newsletter (Association for Gerontology in Higher Education)
AICS Compass (Association of Independent Colleges and Schools)
AIR Newsletter (Association for Institutional Research)
Antaeus Report (Center for the Study of Education and Society Association
    Trends)
APPA Newsletter (Association of Physical Plan Administrators of Universities
    and Colleges)
Association Trends
AVCC Education Newsletter (Australian Vice-Chancellor's Committee)
Behavior Sciences Newsletter (American Institute for Research)
British Open University Foundation, Inc.
Brookings Bulletin (Brookings Institution)
Bulletin (Association of College Unions)
Bulletin (Education Commission of the States)
Bulletin (National Center for Educational Brokering)
CAEL Newsletter (Cooperative Assessment of Experiential Learning)
Campus Report (University of Illinois)
Canadian Society for the Study of Higher Education Newsletter
Career Currents (Wisconsin Career Information System)
CAPE Outlook (Council for American Private Education)
Carnegie Quarterly (Carnegie Foundation)
CASC Newsletter (Council for the Advancement of Small Colleges)
CAUSE Information
CB Report (Texas College and University System)
CCHE (Colorado Commission on Higher Education)
CEW Newsletter (Center for Continuing Education of Women, University
    of Michigan)
CFAE Newsletter (Council for Financial Aid to Education)
Christian College News Service (Christian College Consortium)
Chronicle of Higher Education
CIC Independent (Council of Independent Colleges)
CMA Exchange (Colleges of Mid-America)
Colleague (United Methodist Board of Higher Education and Ministry)
College Board Review News (College Entrance Examination Board)
College and University Business Officers (NACUBO)
Commission on Higher Education Newsletter (Middle States Association of Colleges
    and Schools)
Committee on the Future of International Studies (University of Texas)
Communicator (Council of Graduate Schools in the U.S.)
Communique (American Association of University Administrators)
Council Notes (State Council of Higher Education for Virginia)
Cross-Cultural Southwest Ethnic Study Center (University of Texas)
CUA Newsletter (Conference of University Administrators)
Danforth News and Notes (Danforth Foundation)

Figure 3. Newsletters Focusing on the Field of Higher Education

(continued)

Dialogue on Campus (Association for the Coordination of University
    Religious Affairs)
Digest (State University of New York)
D & R Report (Council for Educational Development and Research)
Educational Researcher (American Educational Research Association)
Education Recaps (Educational Testing Service)
Engineering Manpower Bulletin (Engineers Joint Council)
ETS Development (Educational Testing Service)
Faculty Newsletter (University of Illinois)
Financial Aid News (College Scholarship Service)
Ford Foundation Letter (Ford Foundation)
Forum for Liberal Education (Association of American Colleges)
Forum (National Clearinghouse for Bilingual Education)
FYI (National Association of State Universities and Land-Grant Colleges)
Graduate Bulletin (Syracuse University)
HERDSA News (The Higher Education Research & Development Society
    of Australasia)
Higher Education and Ministry Report (Board of Higher Education and Ministry,
    United Methodist Church)
Higher Education and National Affairs (American Council on Education)
Higher Education Daily (Capitol Publications, Inc.)
Higher Education in Connecticut (Commission on Higher Education)
Higher Education in Europe (European Center for Higher Education, UNESCO)
Higher Education in New England (New England Board of Higher Education)
Higher Education in the States (Education Commission of the States)
Higher Education News Notes (National Council of Churches of Christ in
    the U.S.A.)
Higher Education Report (State Council of Higher Education for Virginia)
IIEP Bulletin (International Institute for Educational Planning [UNESCO])
Illinois Trustee (Illinois Community College Trustee Association)
Imprimis (Center for Constructive Alternatives, Hillsdale College)
Information from Heath/Closer Look (Resource Center)
Innotech Newsletter (SEAMEO Center for Educational Innovation and Technology,
    Philippines)
Innovative Developments (Clearinghouse for Innovative Developments)
Insights (Interpreting Institutes)
Institute for Social Research Newsletter (University of Michigan)
Intercultural Education (International Council for Educational Development)
International Association of Universities Bulletin
IRTHE (Institute for Research & Training in Higher Education, University
    of Cincinnati)
Issues of Higher Education (Southern Regional Education Board)
Items (Social Science Research Council)
Learning Times (College Entrance Examination Board)
Legislative Review (Education Commission of the States)
LULAC News (League of United Latin American Citizens)
Management Forum (Academy for Educational Development)
Maryland Research Chronicle (University of Maryland)
Memo to the President (American Association of State Colleges and Universities)
MHECB Report (Minnesota Higher Education Coordinating Board)
Minnesota State College System Newsletter (Chancellor's Office)
Missing Link (Louisiana Dissemination Network [R&D])
NACS Confidential Bulletin (National Association of College Stores)
NAEP (Education Commission of the States)

Figure 3. Newsletters Focusing on the Field of Higher Education
(continued)

NAEP Newsletter (National Center for Education Statistics)
NAFSA Newsletter (National Association for Foreign Student Affairs)
NASFAA Newsletter (National Association of Student Financial Aid Administrators)
National Center for the Study of Collective Bargaining in Higher Education
  (Baruch College, CUNY)
National Inservice Network Newsletter (National Inservice Network)
National Report for Training and Development (American Society for Training
  and Development)
National Science Foundation News
NCHEMS Newsletter (National Center for Higher Education Management
  Systems)
News from SCUP (Society for College and University Planning)
Newsletter (American Association of Podiatric Medicine)
Newsletter (Association of American Law Schools)
Newsletter (Association of Urban Universities)
Newsletter (Center for Continuing Education for Women)
Newsletter (Council of Europe)
Newsletter (European Cultural Foundation)
Newsletter (Twentieth Century Fund)
News Report (National Academy of Sciences, Research Council)
NJ Interact (New Jersey Department of Education)
Northwest SIMC Newsletter (Northwest Regional Special Instructional Materials
  Center)
Ontario University Program for Instructional Development Newsletter
  (Ontario University)
Organization of Chinese American Women Speaks
Phi Kappa Phi Newsletter
Proceedings Newsletter (Southern Association of Colleges & Schools)
Project on the Status and Education of Women (Association of American Colleges)
PSCCUNY Clarion (Professional Staff Congress, CUNY)
Record (Maryland State Board of Higher Education)
Regional Action (Southern Regional Education Board)
Reports (Council on Postsecondary Accreditation)
Reports on Higher Education (Western Interstate Commission on
  Higher Education)
Research and Development in Postsecondary Education (Office of the Chancellor
  of the Swedish Commission)
Research Corporation Quarterly Bulletin
Research in Education (Scottish Council for Research in Education)
Resource (Newsletter of the Instructional Resource Center, CUNY)
Retain (Drake University's Retention Newsletter)
RF Illustrated (Rockefeller Foundation)
RIHED News (Regional Institute of Higher Education and Development)
RISE (Research and Information Services for Education)
Russell Sage Foundation News
Scholarship, Fellows, and Loans News Service
Science Resources Studies Highlights (National Science Foundation)
Search (Report from the Urban Institute)
SHEEO/NCES Communication Network News (State Higher Education Executive
  Officers/National Center for Education Statistics)
Social Work Education Reporter (Council on Social Work Education, Inc.)
Spotlight (College Placement Council)
Speaking for PHEAA (Pennsylvania Higher Education Assistance Agency)
SSIE Science Newsletter (Smithsonian Science Information Exchange)

Figure 3. Newsletters Focusing on the Field of Higher Education
(continued)

Staff Report (Association of University Programs in Health Administration)
System Summary (University of Georgia)
Teaching (Stanford Center for Research and Development)
Teaching News (University of Birmingham, England)
UMA Update (University of Mid-America)
UME Letter (United Ministries in Education)
Union Wire (Association of College Unions)
Universitas (University Professors for Academic Order)
University Affairs (Association of Universities and Colleges of Canada)
Women's Studies Newsletter (Clearinghouse on Women's Studies)

Note: This list is used by the ERIC Clearinghouse for Higher Education in their publication acquisition for the ERIC monthly bibliographic journal, *Resources in Education.*

Figure 4. Publication Scanned for the Trends Assessment Program, American Council of Life Insurance

Across the Board
Administrative Management
Advertising Age
Aging
Aging & Work
American Banker
American Bar Association Journal
American Demographics
American Health
American Medical News
American Scholar
American Scientist
Architectural Record
Atlantic Monthly

Behavior Today
Brain Mind Bulletin
Brookings Review
Bulletin of Atomic Scientists
Business & Society Review
Business Horizons
The Business Quarterly
Business Week

California Management Review
Canadian Business & Science
Center Magazine
Change — Magazine of Higher Education
Channels
Chronicle of Higher Education
Christian Science Monitor
CoEvolution Quarterly
Columbia Journalism Review

Daedalus
Datamation
Discover
Dun's Business Monthly

East West Journal
The Economist
Emerging Trends (religious issues)

Family Planning Perspectives
Financial Planner
Financial Times
Footnotes to the Future
Forbes
Foreign Affairs
Fortune
Free Lance
Futures
Future Society
The Futurist

Geo
The Gerontologist

Harpers'
Harvard Business Review
Harvard Medical Letter
Hastings Center Report
High Technology
Humanist

Industry Week
In These Times
Institute of Noetic Sciences Newsletter

Figure 4. Publication Scanned for the Trends Assessment Program, American Council of Life Insurance *(continued)*

Journal of Business Strategy
Journal of Communication
Journal of Consumer Affairs
Journal of Contemporary Business
Journal of Insurance
Journal of Long Range Planning
Journal of Social Issues

Leading Edge

Management World
Medical Economics
Medical World News
Money Magazine
Monthly Labor Review
Mother Jones
Ms.

New Age
Nation's Business
New England Journal of Medicine
New Republic
New Scientist
New Times
New York Review of Books
New York Times
Newsweek
Nuclear Times

Off Our Backs
Omni

Personal Computing
Personnel Journal
Policy Studies Review
The Progressive
Psychology Today
Public Opinion
Public Interest
Public Relations Journal

Rain
Resurgence
Rolling Stone

Quest

Saturday Night
Saturday Review
Savvy
Science
Science and Public Policy
Science Digest
Science 82
Science News
The Sciences (New York Academy of Sciences)
Science Technology & Human Values
Scientific American
Sloan Management Review
Smithsonian
Social Policy
Society
Solar Age

Tarrytown Letter
Technology Forecasts
Technology Illustrated
Technology Review
Time
To The Point

Urban Futures Idea Exchange
USA Today
US News & World Report

Vital Speeches of the Day

Wall Street Journal
Washington Monthly
The Wharton
What's Next
The Wilson Quarterly
World Future Society Bulletin
Working Papers for a New Society
Working Woman
World Press Review

include the *New York Times*, with its focus on international affairs; the *Washington Times* or the *Washington Post* with their focus on domestic political developments; the *Chicago Tribune*, with its focus on the Midwest; the *Los Angeles Times*, with its West Coast perspective; and one of the major papers from the Sun Belt (Atlanta, Houston, or Miami). The national perspective, of course, should be supported by a review of the major state, regional, and local newspapers.

Magazines, periodicals, newsletters, and specialized newspapers in each of the four major areas—social, technical, economic, and legislative and regulatory change—should be included. Moreover, publications of special-interest groups attempting to put their issues on the national agenda (Congresswatch, Fusion) and publications by the Union of Concerned Scientists, the Sierra Club, the National Organization for Women, and Phyllis Schlafly's Eagle Forum should also be included. Journals reporting new developments, such as the *Swedish Journal of Social Change* and *Psychology Today*, should be scanned, too.

In addition, a special effort should be made to seek "fringe" publications—the so-called underground press, as exemplified by *The Village Voice* and other nonestablishment publications. Depending on the results of scanning the literature already covered by committee members, a special effort may be necessary to include such publications as *Ms., Glamour, Working Woman, Working Mother, Family Today,* and *The Ladies' Home Journal.* (For those who think the relevance of these publications to higher education is a bit farfetched, we recommend a review of the October 1982 issue of *Glamour*, where, on page 49, one may read the results of their reader's opinions about a proposed cut in student financial aid. While in no way scientific, such opinion polls often are important bellwethers of evolving public opinion and should be considered as significant input into the scanning process and be marked for automatic inclusion into the filing system. Corporations have learned the value of monitoring public opinion and spend tens of thousands of dollars to subscribe to the Lou Harris, Roper, and Gallup polls. Finally, the scanning literature should include a few wild cards—such as *High Times, Corporate Crime Comics, Mother Jones,* and so on. Staffers should maintain lists of publications that are being scanned, with the names of members responsible for scanning them. Obviously, such lists cannot be as large as the one used by Congress, but might easily reach twenty new publications in addition to those already being covered.

Additional resources for scanning include trade and professional publications, association newsletters, conference schedules, and publications of societies and associations in parallel industries. For example, many instructional innovations now occur in the training programs of corporations and are discussed at the annual meeting of American Society for Training and Development and in such publications as *Journal of Training and Development* and *Training: The Magazine of Human Resources Development.* And, as we know, the consumer movement and the concept of strategic planning both developed in the business sector years before most of us in higher education were aware of them as potentially affecting our institutions. Other parallel industries to monitor are health care and social services. For example, Morgan (1983) discusses cost-containment strategies in the health care sector, strategies that may well merit adoption by higher education as funding support lessens.

There are also associations and societies tracking, following, or advocating social change. The World Future Society, for example, publishes *The Futurist, The World Future Society Bulletin*, and *Future Survey*, all dedicated to the exploration and discussion of new ideas and trends about the future. AAHE publishes *Telescan*. The American Council of Life Insurance publishes a newsletter, *Straws in the Wind*, as well as periodic reports on emerging issues, called *The ACLI Trend Report*. In addition, there are commercial services that major corporations use to supplement their scanning functions: the World Future Society's *Future Survey* ($65 per year), Yankelovich's *Corporate Priorities* ($10,000 per year), the Policy Analysis Company's *Congress Scan* ($198 per year), the Naisbitt's Group's *The Trend Report* ($15,000 per year), and SRI International's *Scan* ($5,000 per year). These more expensive outside resources are naturally beyond the range of most college and university budgets and are not without their own liabilities. These services are generic and attempt to cover all issues from all perspectives; even as supplemental resources, they cannot cover the perspective needed for institutional scanning. Overemphasis on outside resources also violates an organizational requirement that the scanning function be indigenous to the existing structure, rather than added on from outside.

The scanning staff should make a special effort to include within the scanning process whatever fugitive literature it is able to obtain. Such literature is not published in the established journals and is available only if its existence is known and it is hunted down. It is, in the truest sense, fugitive. For example, it would include the more than twenty-five articles, pamphlets, and other private publications on the new field of issues management; private publications on changing social values, such as the recent Connecticut Mutual Life Insurance publication; the publications of the Center for Futures Research at the University of Southern California; literature reporting on values and life-styles from SRI International; and so forth. Often, fugitive literature will eventually enter the established literature, but only years after its initial publication. Therefore, it is necessary to develop personal and professional contacts to tap into the fugitive literature network. Professional associations like the Issues Management Association and the North American Society for Corporate Planning, and their conferences, are major resources for fugitive literature.

Other Resources

The scanning committee should tap the resources of its resident experts. This is best done by publishing a weekly or monthly scanning newsletter prepared by the staff. This one- to two-page newsletter presents two to five items from the committee. Such newsletters continue to build a constituency for the scanning process as well as an informal network for recognition and appreciation of the scanning results. The newsletter might be sent, for example, to all department chairs along with an open invitation for their comments and contributions of new ideas that they see in their fields. Colleges and universities are in a unique position to conduct scanning processes; other organizations cannot call upon the breadth and depth of experience available on most faculties.

Internal scanning newsletters often use political and issue cartoons found in major newspapers and in national magazines like *The New Yorker*. These issue cartoons provide an important signal that an issue has reached national standing and that some consensus on the issue exists. These cartoons serve the additional function of communicating a tremendous amount of information in a very small space. Most pioneering scanning newsletters make regular use of such cartoons.

Final Comment

After a year in operation, the scanning staff should begin to develop a schedule for regular review and updating of the files and to maintain a record of this review process. The staff should also maintain the files, opening and closing file categories only with the approval of the whole committee, and not in response to pressure from any one person or group of persons on the committee or on the basis of the special interests of the scanning staff.

Between meetings of the scanning committee, the scanning staff person will compile all the suggestions and items forwarded from all sources. Before the meeting, the scanning staffer should review these materials with a small subcommittee and prepare lists of input materials for the full scanning committee. This preliminary screening saves the entire committee from having to consider five or six different items that all suggest the same issue. The subcommittee meeting should result in a list of twenty to thirty items for the full committee to consider. The chair or the director of institutional research is responsible for all the background materials necessary to support discussion. The scanning files will obviously grow over time, placing tremendous importance on the continuing review process.

References

Aguilar, F. J. *Scanning the Business Environment.* New York: Macmillan, 1967.
Morgan, A. W. "Cost as a Policy Issue: Lessons for the Health Care Sector." *Journal of Higher Education,* 1983, *54* (3), 279–293.

William L. Renfro is president of Policy Analysis Company, Inc., 148 E Street, S.E., Washington, D.C. 20003. He is issues management editor of The Futurist *and serves on the board of directors of the Issues Management Association.*

James L. Morrison is professor of education at the University of North Carolina, Chapel Hill. He is on the board of directors of the Association for the Study of Higher Education and serves as chair of the Special Interest Group on Futures Research, American Educational Research Association.

Attempting to forecast the most likely future for higher education
may be an exercise in futility, but developing detailed descriptions of
alternative futures can be useful for making desirable futures happen.

Judgmental Forecasting
Techniques and Institutional
Planning: An Example

Peter H. Wagschall

That the 1980s represent a crucial decade for American higher education is, to say the least, a vast understatement. This decade will be the one in which declining enrollments — resulting from the end of the baby boom in 1965 — make their first impact on America's colleges and universities. Indeed, the graduating class of 1987 will be the first in the past eighteen years to be drawn from a non–baby boom cohort. But the 1980s are also clearly the decade of the electronic revolution, a set of changes in information handling that are so extraordinary and far-reaching as to leave most futurists gasping at the possibilities. And, to complicate an already muddied future, this decade will continue to be characterized by a troubled global and national economy, public uncertainty over the quality and value of higher education, ever aging college faculties, and mounting pressures from industry for properly trained personnel.

In the midst of such uncertainty and rapidly paced change, it is no longer enough for us to insist that our institutions of higher education begin to take the task of long-range forecasting more seriously. Similar calls to arms have been heard all too frequently in the past; and while they have often resulted in lengthy planning documents, they have all too rarely led to identifi-

J. L. Morrison, W. L. Renfro, and W. I. Boucher (Eds.) *Applying Methods and Techniques of Futures Research.*
New Directions for Institutional Research, no. 39. San Francisco: Jossey-Bass, September 1983.

able improvements in the quality of either research or instruction in higher education. Forecasting any aspect of the future is no mean feat, especially in times as fluid as these, but there is something particularly frustrating about such exercises when they are conducted by colleges and universities. Woodrow Wilson, for example, was once asked to compare the politics of the American presidency with the politics of Princeton University. He remarked that the university was far more complex. And — at least so the story goes — it was only when they found the complexities of Massachusetts Institute of Technology too frustrating to simulate by computer that Donnella and Dennis Meadows and their colleagues (1972) turned their attention to a more simple project — the global simulations of limits to growth.

In fact, attempts at long-range planning in higher education have been plagued more frequently by dissent and dilution than by errors of judgment. Rarely has a college or a university invested heavily in a set of plans that simply turned out to be wrong in its basic forecasts of the future; instead, lengthy plans are made only to be watered down to appease a faculty union, to suit the tastes of a new president, or to avoid alienating influential alumni. Likewise, bold initiatives are started, only to be scuttled because faculty members, administrators, alumni, or commercial allies develop the political clout to block measures that they believe not to be in their own best interests. Perhaps more than any other institution in America, colleges and universities require long-range planning that promotes agreement among diverse factions right from the start. The most technically correct and expertly prepared forecast, if developed without the involvement of key personnel from all sectors of higher education, is virtually certain to be ignored.

The planning processes described in this chapter are focused less on the attempt to forecast higher education futures accurately than on the need to gain consensus among potential planners. The scenarios resulting from these processes gain their value not from some objective estimate of their validity but from the commitment and involvement of the participants. Indeed, this process — called *futuring* — has already enabled at least two groups of public school educators to begin redesigning their programs for what they see as the needs of the coming century. The New York State Department of Education's futuring project in occupational and practical arts, which began in May 1981, is now developing detailed curricular materials based on a shared view of the future. In New York State, futuring has enabled teachers, state department of education administrators, local school administrators, and major corporation executives to come to unanimous agreement regarding the most appropriate goals and strategies for occupational and practical arts education over the coming two decades. Similarly, the Massachusetts State Department of Education's Adult Basic Education Division currently uses futuring as a way of gaining agreement on the most promising directions for adult basic education over the remainder of this century.

Futuring—An Overview

The key to futuring is the development of richly detailed descriptions of alternative futures. It is easy to lose sight of the overall process while describing any one of the elements of futuring. The general outlines of futuring (as it applies, say, to planning the future of a particular university) can be described in the following manner.

1. Perhaps the most crucial element is establishing the appropriate planning group. In the case of developing a long-range plan for a university, this group must include representatives of all factions that may have a substantial stake in the resulting plan—faculty members, administrators, students, boards of trustees, legislators, corporate executives, alumni, and possibly governmental agencies at all levels. This group will be required to put in approximately three days of work during the planning process. It should include individuals in prominent positions who are capable of representing as well as leading their various constituencies. Since group members will have to interact vigorously when they are working, the total group should probably not exceed twenty participants.

2. The planning group meets for approximately one day. The futuring process as a whole is described, and an assortment of expert futurists can be brought in to stimulate thinking about relevant possible, probable, and preferable trends over the next twenty to thirty years. Following these presentations, the group spends two hours brainstorming as many trends and events as it can, covering the gamut of developments that need to be taken into account in the long-range plan.

3. The results of the brainstorming session are boiled down to a set of no more than fifty items, which serve as the basis for a Delphi questionnaire. This questionnaire is mailed in three rounds to a group of at least a hundred people representing those constituents whose need either to approve or to be involved in the ultimate plan is most crucial. In the case of a university, this group should include students, faculty members, administrators, legislators, business leaders, members of the board of trustees, alumni, key government officials at all levels, experts in higher education, and possibly others.

4. The results of the Delphi questionnaire are tabulated and presented to the planning group, which selects three very important trends as the focus for its work in developing six "futures wheels." In the course of one six-hour meeting, the planning group completes the futures wheels by dividing into working groups of from five to seven people. Each completed wheel is likely to have at least 120 probable consequences of the most likely and important trends under consideration.

5. For each trend, a cross-impact matrix is developed for rough informal estimations of the likely interactions among the 120 or so consequences. This process results in a ranking of consequences for each trend, wherein some

are rated as extremely likely to occur and others are judged as extremely unlikely.

6. These collections of consequences serve as the basis for the writing of from six to eighteen scenarios, each of which describes in some detail a possible future for the university. The planning group meets for one more day to review the scenarios, make whatever modifications seem appropriate, and select those most accurately reflecting the group's combined judgments of the most likely and beneficial futures for the university.

To be sure, this description of futuring leaves out far more than it includes, but the general outline above does indicate some of the key features of the process. First, this planning process relies heavily on combined intuitions, common sense, and personal judgments. While some statistical manipulations are involved—for example, in the Delphi questionnaires and the cross-impact matrix—the process is mostly grounded in the shared, intuitive understandings of the participants. Second, futuring involves planners in an alternating series of expanding and contracting exercises enabling them to think both more concretely and more comprehensively about the future. Planners begin with brainstorming, an expansive process, and then proceed to a Delphi questionnaire, which narrows the diversity of alternative trends to a manageable few. Next, they are involved in another expansive process—the futures wheel—only to proceed to the convergence-based cross-impact matrix. Finally, futuring is discrete, manageable, and not excessively time-consuming. Since it has a beginning and an end, it can be separated from the numerous other day-to-day planning activities in which any institution must engage. Depending on the level of energy devoted to it, a full futuring process, such as the one described above, can be completed within as short a time as six months; only rarely will it take more than a year.

Futuring—A Concrete Example

Futuring is a local process designed to assist particular groups and institutions in planning their own futures, and so any general description is unlikely to convey its specific nature. The following example is intended to give a more detailed look at futuring, but a few caveats are necessary. First, this example was developed as part of a graduate seminar; hence, it does not reflect the crucial, consensus-producing aspects of futuring. Unlike contexts in which futuring may be used to guide real decisions, the following example was essentially an academic exercise. While it explains the components of futuring, it does not have the action orientation central to futuring as an aid to institutional planning. Second, this example is abbreviated, with each component carried out only as far as is necessary for describing the techniques involved; describing a fully implemented futuring exercise obviously would take far more space than this chapter allows.

The Brainstorm

Our example began with brainstorming of trends and events that may affect higher education over the coming twenty years. Approximately one hour was spent in brainstorming according to what are by now fairly standard rules; that is, all possibilities were encouraged and no criticism was allowed. The session resulted in a list of over fifty trends and events covering a fairly diverse territory. Some had to do with the external environment of higher education: *decline in the age group between eighteen and twenty-one; increasing energy costs; widespread use of home computers.* Other trends focused on potential changes in higher education's clients: *more older students; more minority students; more women in math and science.* Several of the identified trends centered on financial matters: *smaller budgets; increasing tuition; increased cost per student.* Still others had to do with potential changes in the structure of higher education: *elimination of tenure; more cooperation with private industry; increased use of computers as teachers.*

Given the time limitations in our seminar, the trends were grouped and assessed by the seminar members, but in any real application the futuring would have called for a Delphi questionnaire at this point.

As outlined earlier, the identified trends should yield a list of no more than fifty. These fifty trends then become the basis for a questionnaire in which respondents are asked to assess both the likelihood and the importance of each trend. Using the present example, one of the questions on such a Delphi might be: *"Tenure is eliminated:* How likely is this to occur within the next twenty years? (1 = very unlikely; 2 = unlikely; 3 = possible; 4 = likely; 5 = very likely) If this were to occur, how extensive would its impact on higher education be? (1 = very significant; 2 = significant; 3 = moderate; 4 = insignificant; 5 = very insignificant)."

After the questionnaires are returned, the mean answer for each question is determined, and then it is mailed again to the same people. On this second round, each respondent is told the mean answer of the group, as well as his or her own previous answer to each item, and asked to respond again. This entire process is repeated a third time.

When the third-round Delphi questionnaires have been returned and the mean answer has been determined for each question, there will be substantially more unanimity in the answers; the range and standard deviation will be smaller than they were in the first round. By removing the opportunity for face-to-face contact (and, hence, the possibility for people with different opinions to defend their positions), the Delphi questionnaire tends to move its respondents toward unanimity on whatever issues it raises. Thus, at the end of the third round of the Delphi process, respondents will have identified the trends that they believe will be most likely, and most significant in their impact on higher education, over the coming twenty years. It is important to note here that this unanimity may have no relationship to reality: Our respondents could all agree and all be very wrong; but their agreement is an accurate reflection of their present sentiments. Hence, agreement is the best starting point for respondents planning jointly for the future, as they see it. Moreover, the fairly high degree of agreement produced by the Delphi is invaluable in developing plans for higher education, where, as we have already seen, factionalism is often the most serious obstacle to any attempt at long-range planning.

The Futures Wheel

Once the most likely and most important trends have been identified through a Delphi questionnaire, the next stage is to draw out the consequences of those trends in richer detail. In our seminar, we selected *tenure is eliminated* as an event both important and likely enough to be worth exploring, and we proceeded to look at the potential consequences of such a major change.

The rules for constructing a futures wheel are essentially opposite the those of a brainstorming session: Any individual in the group may propose a consequence of the original item (in our case, *tenure is eliminated*), but all other members of the group have veto power. If any member thinks that the proposed consequence will not occur, it is eliminated and another consequence is proposed. In developing detailed descriptions helpful for institutional planning, it is probably best to begin with four consequences of the original trend. For lack of time, however, we settled on the following three: *academic quality of faculty improves; reduction in personnel costs; more frequent turnover of faculty.*

Each of these consequences then becomes the center of its own wheel. The search for consequences continues, following precisely the same rules, with any group member able to veto any proposed consequence. When three unanimously agreed-upon consequences have been developed for each of the Level 1 consequences, then Level 2 is completed. In our case, the wheel at Level 2 looked like Figure 1.

Once our Level 2 was completed, each of its nine consequences became the center of its own wheel; thus, there were twenty-seven consequences at Level 3. In our example, the twenty-seven Level 3 consequences were as follows, beginning with their Level 2 antecedents:

> *Improved learning experiences:* students enjoy learning; cumulative averages increase; graduate school enrollments increase. *More research accomplished:* faculty publications increase; more research labs are built; more postdoctoral positions are available. *Students more satisfied with their education:* Students enjoy learning; graduates are more successful in their careers; respect for faculty increases. *Faculty unions get stronger:* salaries of faculty increase; faculty's political power increases; administration of higher education becomes more difficult. *More funds for non-*

Figure 1. A Futures Wheel: Consequences of Tenure Elimination

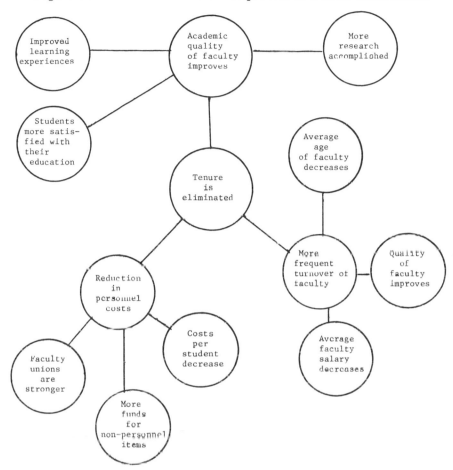

personnel items: recreational opportunities increase; more student services; more money for support services. *Costs per student decrease:* more
students enroll; more minorities enroll; parents are happier. *Average age
of faculty decreases:* student–faculty ideals and values are more compatible; average faculty salary decreases; innovative ideas of faculty
increase. *Quality of faculty improves:* use of educational technologies
increases; average GRE scores increase; more research funds are
awarded. *Average faculty salaries decrease:* faculty consulting increases;
ratio of faculty to students improves; tuitions increase less rapidly.

Finally, the process of deriving still other consequences from these
consequences continues for one more round, with the above twenty-seven

consequences serving as the starting point for the eighty-one consequences of Level 4. Space does not allow a full description of our example's Level 4, but a few examplary consequences follow, with their Level 3 antecedents:

> *Student/faculty ideals and values more compatible:* mutual satisfaction with curriculum; average GPAs increase; learning is more enjoyable. *Average faculty salary decreases:* more faculty spouses are employed; faculty moonlighting increases; more-qualified faculty members leave the profession. *Innovative ideas of faculty increase:* increase in new technology; more grant funds available; professional image of faculty is enhanced. *Use of educational technologies increases:* cost of higher education decreases; technological sophistication of graduates increases; instructional processes employ more computers.

Upon completion of this "three-by-four" futures wheel (that is, three consequences at each level, and four levels), we produced 120 possible consequences of our original trend, *tenure is eliminated.* Each consequence had the unanimous vote of confidence of our planning group, since all vetoed possibilities were eliminated. Thus, the 120 statements represented our group's best consensus on what would happen to our institution if tenure were eliminated.

Several common features of futures wheels are worth noting. First, the process can proceed quite rapidly so long as the veto prerogative is explained clearly and enforced rigidly. Time should not be devoted to arguing about the likelihood of any particular consequence. If any one person is hesitant at all about its likelihood, then it should be eliminated, and other possibilities explored. The wheel used in our example was developed by six people in less than two hours. Second, consequences (especially at Levels 3 and 4) are often surprising, sometimes repetitive, and occasionally contradictory. In our example, we have *average faculty salary decreases* at Level 3 and *salaries increase* also at Level 3, deriving from different antecedents. Since the futures wheel is an expansive process, these duplications and contradictions are to be expected; in fact, they reflect the power of this technique. In a society as complex as ours, it is clear that even the most simple trends exert a variety of influences on the institutions and trends around them, often leading to contradictory pressures.

In practice, it is important to make sure that the search for consequences at each level proceeds quickly and that the process is carried out through Level 4, where some of the more interesting and surprising consequences usually appear.

The Cross-Impact Matrix

Having expanded our vision of what the university might be like if tenure were eliminated, we needed some way of organizing the diverse consequences we created. A simple version of a cross-impact matrix can serve this purpose. In our use of this method, we arranged the consequences in a 120-by-120 matrix. For each box of the matrix we asked, "If the trend on the left were to occur, what impact — negative or positive — would it have on the trends listed across the top?" These questions can be asked informally by relying on the combined judgments of group members (as was done for the futures wheel and placing *0* where there is disagreement). They also can be asked more formally by investigating the research literature to see what the past relationships have been among similar trends. For our example, the process was completed informally and, thus, in a very short time. When used as part of a real planning process, the informal approach would serve only as a starting point. A portion of the cross-impact matrix from our example, including nine of our final consequences is shown in Figure 2. The " – – " in the second box of the first row, for example, indicates our judgment that *decline in average faculty salaries* would have a *very negative* impact on the tendency for *innovative ideas to increase*. For another example, the " + (single plus) in the second box of the seventh row indicates our judgment that faculty off-campus consulting increases would have a positive (but not very positive) impact on the tendency for innovative ideas to increase.

Once each box of the matrix has been filled in, the data in the columns and rows can be aggregated in several ways. For example, they can be added algebraically to obtain a measure of the overall effect of the occurence or nonoccurence of other trends in the set. Thus, the numbers shown at the end of each row measure the extent to which the trends on the left are estimated to have a positive or negative impact on the other trends in the set. As these numbers indicate, the first trend (average faculty salary declines) produces the greatest negative changes, while trend six (use of educational technology increases) produces the greatest positive changes. The numbers shown at the bottom of the columns indicate the extent that each of the trends listed across the top of the matrix are positively or negatively affected by other trends in the set. For example, both trends two and six are influenced most positively by the occurrence of other trends, while the last trend (tuition increases less rapidly) is not affected at all.

Scenario Writing

With our cross-impact matrix completed, it was possible to group our consequences according to their likelihood and then write a series of scenarios reflecting our group's judgment of what would happen to the university if tenure were eliminated. For our very abbreviated example, we can summarize that the most likely description of a university without tenure would include the following consequences: *Innovative ideas have increased; research funds have*

Figure 2. A Cross-Impact Matrix: Consequences of Tenure Elimination

	Average faculty salary declines	Innovative ideas increase	Student–faculty ideals more compatible	Research funds increase	Average GREs increase	Use of educational technologies increases	Faculty off-campus consulting increases	Faculty–student ratio improves	Tuition increases less rapidly	Sum of impacts
Average faculty salary declines	X	− −	0	− −	0	−	0	0	0	4 −
Innovative ideas increase	− −	X	0	+ +	+	+ +	+	+	0	5 +
Student–faculty ideals more compatible	0	+	X	0	+	0	0	+	0	3 +
Research funds increase	−	+ +	0	X	0	+	+ +	0	0	5 +
Average GREs increase	0	+	+	0	X	+	0	+	0	4 +
Use of educational technology increases	0	+ +	0	+ +	+	X	+	0	−	6 +
Faculty off-campus consulting increases	+ +	+	−	+	0	+	X	0	0	5 +
Faculty–student ratio improves	0	0	0	−	0	0	−	X	−	0
Tuition increases less rapidly	+	0	0	0	0	−	0	0	X	1 +
Sum of impacts	1 +	5 +	1 +	3 +	3 +	5 +	4 +	3 +	0	

increased; average GRE scores have increased; the use of educational technology has increased; faculty off-campus consulting has increased; the faculty–student ratio has improved. An alternative but less likely scenario would be one with these consequences: *average faculty salaries have declined; student–faculty ideals are more compatible; tuition increases less rapidly.*

It is probably worth noting here that, somewhat surprisingly, the impact that elimination of tenure would have on academic freedom never came up in our discussions, primarily because there was no consensus that any real relationship exists between these two factors. It is also noteworthy that full implementation of a futuring process with *tenure is eliminated* as an event to be investigated (via futures wheels, the cross-impact matrix, and scenario writing) would include at least sixty statements in the *most likely* category.

Creating Alternative Futures

There are many reasons and methods for studying the future, and the processes outlined here as futuring are not intended to serve them all. Futuring is not, for example, suitable for attempts to determine what is most likely to happen to unemployment rates over the coming decade, nor is it necessarily the best approach in any realm. But futuring does allow for a systematic consideration of alternative futures in a way that few institutions have yet attempted. Futuring enables us to ask, "What would happen to us if. . .?" and then answer that question with a unanimity and concreteness rare in institutions of higher education. Most important, futuring enables us to answer such questions in a reasonably short time and to produce specific and fairly unanimous scenarios that can serve us as the basis for creating genuine alternatives to our present practices.

Reference

Meadows, D. H., Meadows, D. L., Randers, J., and Behrens, W. W., III. *The Limits to Growth: A Report for the Club of Rome's Project on the Predicament of Mankind.* New York: Universe Books, 1972.

Peter H. Wagschall is director of the futures study program at the University of Massachusetts, Amherst, and he is currently directing a commission funded by Phi Delta Kappa International that will produce a handbook on schooling for the 21st century.

Multiple scenario analysis addresses the dilemma of strategic planners who must have some understanding of the future while recognizing the inadequacy of predicting it.

Multiple Scenario Analysis: Introducing Uncertainty into the Planning Process

Richard B. Heydinger
Rene D. Zentner

However good our futures research may be, we shall never be able to escape from the ultimate dilemma that all of our knowledge is about the past, and all of our decisions are about the future (Wilson, 1974, p. 15).

Nothing is more obvious than the unpredictability of the future. No person of sound mind would choose to debate this point, and yet only within the last decade have planners consciously included the concept of uncertainty in the planning process. Planning staffs typically have presented pictures of a predetermined future, one with obstacles to be overcome and opportunities to be seized. Nevertheless, experience has shown that no such unique forecast can be relied upon. This fact creates a dilemma for strategic planners, who need to

Selected portions of this chapter have appeared in other publications by Mr. Zentner (see the reference section at the end of this chapter). Mr. Heydinger wishes to acknowledge the generous support of the W. K. Kellogg Foundation for the preparation of this chapter.

J. L. Morrison, W. L. Renfro, and W. I. Boucher (Eds.). *Applying Methods and Techniques of Futures Research.* New Directions for Institutional Research, no. 39. San Francisco: Jossey-Bass, September 1983.

have some understanding of future forces while still recognizing that the future cannot be predicted. One way out of this dilemma is to chart a number of possible futures. By adopting this approach, planners can consider a wide range of possible developments — not just the probable, but also the possible. As a result, uncertainty comes to the forefront of planning.

Multiple scenario analysis (MSA) is a relatively new approach to introducing uncertainty into the planning process. In its rudimentary form, the principle underlying the technique is familiar to all of us. For example, athletic teams, in their practice sessions, test their strategies against a number of "what if" situations. This exercise recognizes the indeterminacy of the game and prepares the team for any number of strategies the opponent may employ. Each practice situation is a scenario for the game. Generals also use scenarios in developing military strategies. Scenarios of wars and campaigns that may never be fought are created so that military planners can devise tactics, examine weapons systems, and train their juniors for real wars that may arise.

What Is a Scenario?

The word *scenario* comes from the dramatic arts. In the theatre, it is an outline of the plot; for movies, a scenario sets forth the sequence of action, descriptions of characters and scenes, and other details relevant to the plot, without reproducing the actual script. Herman Kahn, himself no mean showman, introduced the word *scenario* into planning jargon while at the RAND Corporation in the 1950s. The term was used in connection with military and strategic studies conducted by RAND for the government; it subsequently appeared in the late 1960s in a book written by Kahn and Wiener, *The Year 2000*, where scenarios were defined as "Hypothetical sequences of events constructed for the purpose of focusing attention on casual processes and decision points" (1967, p. 8). As a corporate planning tool, scenarios became popular in the early 1970s, when the petroleum industry began to use them to deal with the unpredictability of the Arab oil embargo. Scenarios came to the attention of the general public in 1972, when Dennis and Donnella Meadows published their much debated study, *The Limits to Growth*, which outlined selected scenarios for world resource consumption.

By thinking about the future as multiple scenarios, forecasters deal with ranges of trends and events, not with particular sequences. These ranges can include demographic changes, technological developments, political events, social trends, and economic variables.

Scenarios of the future may take many different forms. A scenario may be a terse outline characterizing the range of assumptions for each major factor to be considered in planning, or these same factors may be described in a thirty-page essay that resembles a short story. A scenario may be exclusively tables or exclusively text; more will be said below on the choice of a scenario format.

In using multiple scenario analysis, it is important to understand its overall role in planning. Scenarios provide a context for planning. They are akin to the already familiar budgeting and enrollment assumptions that often accompany planning instructions, but instead of a single assumption for each planning parameter, a range of assumptions may be considered. In turn, assumptions for different parameters are woven together to form an internally consistent whole, which forms a particular scenario. Two, three, or four scenarios are sometimes developed. Like planning instructions issued by an institution's president, scenarios are distributed as background for new planning cycles.

Multiple scenarios communicate to deans and department chairs, for example, that, while the future is unpredictable, it still must be anticipated. In the strategic planning vernacular, a unit's effective plan is one that can recognize the possibility of any of several scenarios. For instance, in a planning conference with the academic vice-president, a dean or a department chair may be expected to explain how a particular strategy will play itself out if the future generally follows Scenario A. That explanation may be followed by questions relating to Scenario B. Contrast this approach with two other, more traditional formats for planning:

1. Academic units are given budget targets (for example, a 5 percent decline in real resources) and asked to submit plans based on this single assumption. Regardless of how sophisticated the projection techniques are, forecasts based on such budget targets are very unlikely to predict the future accurately. As a result, plans that may have assumed the same immutability of such budget targets are no longer useful, and planners (deans, department chairs) discredit the planning process. This approach communicates an omniscience on the part of the planning staff and the central officers that reality will never bear out.

2. Academic units are asked to develop two sets of plans, one based on a 5 percent decline in resources and one based on a 5 percent increase in resources. Although this directive does communicate uncertainty, academic units recognize that at least one set of plans will be mercly an exercise. Planning thus becomes a kind of charade, and once again the process is easily discredited.

Distributing some manageable number of scenarios to planners has the important effect of letting planners see the different, major dimensions of the future that the administration is considering. This effect is summarized by Edward Cornish: "When we develop a scenario, we free ourselves from strict bondage to the past. No longer are we assuming that the future will be like the past except more so (as in trend extrapolation)" (1977, p. 114).

Two Possible Scenarios for Higher Education

Multiple scenario analysis is more a technique of judgment and art than of science. The guidelines in this chapter resemble general hints that one might give a student for writing a short story more than they resemble the precise rules for constructing a multiple regression model. Like writing a short story, the process of generating scenarios may proceed in any number of ways. But, as with good literature, a body of criticism is developing, which offers guidance to planners interested in using multiple scenario analysis.

Given not only the inexact nature of generating scenarios but also the variety of formats they may assume, two plausible scenarios for higher education are presented in Figures 1A and 1B (see pages 55-57). These are too broad and unspecific for institutional planning purposes, but they do convey the flavor of a scenario.

Scenario Development

Scenarios — unlike single-point forecasts — not only can encompass probable trends or events but also can include highly improbable yet important developments. This point is most easily conveyed by the simple matrix in Figure 2. Likelihood is often the planning variable that receives the most consideration. Equally important, but frequently overlooked, are developments that are extremely important but also unlikely to occur. Multiple scenarios allow organizations to ask planners to consider a whole range of possible environmental conditions.

Figure 2. A Simple Typology for Any Future Development

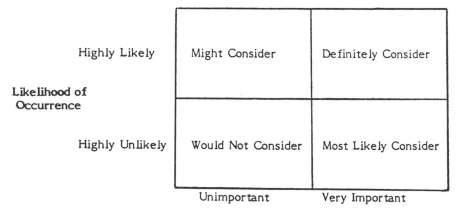

	Unimportant	Very Important
Highly Likely	Might Consider	Definitely Consider
Highly Unlikely	Would Not Consider	Most Likely Consider

Likelihood of Occurrence

Importance to the Organization

Figure 1A. Tooling and Retooling Scenario

Two characteristics drive this scenario. First, the fundamental shift from a manufacturing economy to one based on information processing and on services has continued. New businesses based on these growth segments of our society are formed, while many companies shrink as manufacturing increasingly moves to less developed nations. Rather than a boom or bust economy, it is boom AND bust with businesses in the information and service industries having more job openings than candidates while employees in the manufacturing industries experience high rates of unemployment. Moreover, needed job skills change at an ever quickening pace. Two, three or four career changes in a lifetime is not unusual.

The second driving force is the continued recognition by both industry and students that a college education is the best road to success. If you already have a degree but are seeking a new career, colleges and universities are still viewed as the best source for fundamental job skills. For recent high school graduates, a college degree will not guarantee you a job; however, without a degree you can be guaranteed of not having a job. With required job skills changing rapidly, people find it necessary to return to formal schooling, not only to update themselves in their current profession but to improve their marketability for possible career changes.

These trends have a number of important implications for colleges and universities. Because of those seeking to "retool" for a career change, the feared enrollment decline is mitigated. Overall, nationwide enrollment in colleges and universities falls only 1.5%. Yet the composition of the student body undergoes some fundamental and dramatic shifts. Rather than an enrollment graph which is spiked around the ages of 18-25, a graph of college and university students is now nearly rectangular across the ages of 18-45.

Increasingly students recognize that excellence in the classroom enhances the probability of landing a much sought-after position. This coupled with an increase in the proportion of older students translates into a learning environment in which the students are much more serious about their studies than was true in 1983. As a result students demand high quality instruction. The passive acceptance of poor teaching is a relic of the past, for students know that their marketability depends on high quality training with the latest equipment and techniques. Thus, law suits by students over the misrepresentation of a costly economic good has become commonplace. Faculty members are under increased pressure to offer stimulating and up-to-date classroom material. Because of the greater age span amongst students, there is a wide range of values debated in classroom discussion. As a result classroom interaction has become more heated. The implicit view that the faculty member is somehow superior to the student (leftover from the old days of in loco parentis) has completely disappeared. Faculty who prize the value of the liberal arts find themselves in a smaller and smaller minority, as students focus almost exclusively on the need for vocational skills.

Finally, this scenario assumes that non-higher educational organizations will not enter the market to offer basic vocational training. Although there is fierce competition for the continuing education dollar, giving a person the wide set of skills necessary for a new career remains exclusively the responsibility of traditional colleges and universities.

The current traditionally aged college student wants to "tool-up" to enter the marketplace; the returning college graduate wants to take an already developed set of skills and "re-tool" so that she may take on a second, third, or even fourth career.

Figure 1B. Youth Reject Schooling

Despite all efforts by both private and public sectors the United States continues to slip as an economic and industrial power. The economy continues a slow downward drift as structural unemployment remains in manufacturing and other heavy industry. Some industries continue to expand with job openings prevalent in selected high tech areas (i.e., biogenetics, chemical engineering, cyrogenies) as well as selected skilled trades (i.e., carpentry, electricians, landscape maintenance).

Generally, however, college graduates have an extremely difficult time locating a position which uses their full potential. Salaries for entry level white collar positions are often less than the comparable wage earned by an apprentice carpenter or electrician.

The expectations of a "micro-millenium" have generally been realized with computing and communications playing a significant role in people's personal and professional lives. There has been a veritable explosion of available hardware and software for every facet of activity imaginable. Entertainment and business software with varying levels of sophistication are found in every home and office.

These trends working in concert with each other have led to a situation of grave concern for educators. It is obvious that all but the most elite youth are rejecting (formal) education. There are few job openings which demand a college degree and in which one can expect to earn more than in an "8

The federal government has extricated itself completely from the financial aid business. For any but the wealthy who still view it as in their best interests to obtain a college degree, they must borrow a significant sum of money which will require many years to payback.

With a sluggish economy and public reaction swinging against colleges and universities, higher education has slipped even further on the fiscal agenda of the states. Major research universities are being maintained but nothing more. Many non-selective state institutions have been closed or merged. The worst fears about the future of the non-selective private liberal arts colleges have come to pass; only a few have been able to find their niche in the marketplace. The selective private institutions with significant endowments are vital but not necessarily thriving.

Nearly all of today's students come from at least third generation college families. These students are slated to be in the traditional professions, executives in the major corporations, or entrepreneurs in their own business venture. As a result collegiate studentbodies, in addition to being much smaller, are more homogeneous than any time in the last 30 years. Although there are an equal number of men and women enrolled in postsecondary education, the only racial diversity is a result of an increasing number of foreign students who have enrolled at all levels.

to 5" manual labor position. Thus, there is little motivation to enroll in postsecondary education. Youth are outspoken in their criticism of the poor pedagogical technique used in all aspects of formal schooling whether it be the high school classroom or the college course. Today's youth have been weaned on a steady diet of fast paced information presented in short bursts. They are accustomed to instant feedback and have learned to handle inputs from a variety of stimulii simultaneously. The format of the college course which has changed little over the past century seems archaic to them.

The shifting focus of the 1970s and 80s from concern with professions to concern with avocations has continued. Today's population spends much more time on their hobbies and recreational activities than their counterparts in earlier generations. As a result, a large segment of today's population avoid positions which would infringe on their time away from the office. Finding a manageable and undemanding 8-5 position is a specific objective of many youth as well as older adults.

These societal trends are further exacerbated by the high cost of postsecondary education, which must be borne almost entirely by the family.

Enrollment in all but a few professional programs has dropped precipitously so that there is concern over the growing shortage of advanced degree holders in needed specialities within education, industry, and government.

For those who have decided to enroll, their mood is an odd mixture of devotion to learning coupled with a smugness that belies the fact that meaningful careers most likely await each graduate. College students demand high quality instruction, for like their peers who have opted out of schooling, they too have been exposed to stimulating educational materials and live a fast-paced life style.

Faculty on campuses have a feeling of relief, for they know that for whatever reasons their careers in academe have been spared while many of their graduate school colleagues have been forced out. The mood is one of "minding the store" while waiting for better days ahead. The public's critical attitude toward formal schooling is so overwhelming that individual faculties do not attempt to tackle a societal problem of this magnitude. Instead, a spirit of elitism grows on the college campuses as both faculty and students see themselves creating distance between their own lives and those of the "commoners".

Determination of Purposes and Time Horizon. The first step in developing a scenario is to gain clarity about its purposes and its time frame. A scenario can be used to describe situations that range in scale from all of higher education to individual academic departments. Scenarios have been used for a number of years in the petroleum industry, where the time frame is approximately ten years — the time required to explore, locate, and extract fossil fuels. Thus, the petroleum industry requires ten years to research, decide, act on, and realize the benefits of a particular strategy. In colleges and universities that depend heavily on enrollment for income, the time frame may be fifteen years, a foreseeable horizon with regard to student demography, college attendance rates, and faculty composition. Shorter time frames may be based on the number of years required to plan and execute a major fund-raising campaign or fundamental changes in the composition of the legislature.

In designing scenarios, it must be remembered that social, political, and economic forces move slowly. Thus, public policies do not produce identifiable results in their first few years, public attitudes on issues require years to manifest themselves, and regional or national changes in the economy take extended periods of time. For these reasons, scenarios dealing with such matters at the macro level should be extended for appropriate time periods. Four or five years is generally considered to be the minimum time for scenarios dealing with these topics to unfold, and the decade is a time frame already accepted by commentators as well as their audiences.

Selection of Elements. Scenario development is essentially a process in which elements relevant to the purpose of the scenario are selected from the total environment. While in the real world all variables more or less impinge on human action, scenarios are too limited to embrace all possible variables, and only the most relevant ones can be chosen. In discussing scenarios, five principal areas from which elements will be chosen can be identified: the social, technological, political, economic, and ecological realms. These divisions are useful for categorizing general topic areas, but are relatively useless for identifying particular elements to be selected.

Because higher education has a broad set of purposes and is influenced by many different aspects of society, there is a tendency to be all-encompassing in the selection of scenario elements. Although this tendency may be intellectually attractive, a delicate balance must be struck between limiting choice only to crucial aspects of the environment and ensuring that the variables selected are broad enough to represent the dynamic forces of change affecting colleges and universities. For example, almost every institutional planning scenario will include student demography as one element, with legislative appropriations, federal research contracts, and economic factors possibly included as well. Less obvious, but perhaps equally influential, are such elements as public attitudes about the value of a college degree and influences from developments in telecommunications and information processing. Figure 3 presents a list of potential key elements, with premises; obviously, some of these factors drive others.

In deciding on key elements to include, a scenario author may want to use existing sources of information. For trends relating to society as a whole, myriad statistics are produced by the federal government as well as by private firms (for example, the Chase econometric projections). The volume of this information can be overwhelming, but some private groups offer environmental scanning services (SRI, formerly Stanford Research Institute; The Naisbitt Group; Weiner, Edrich, Brown, Inc.). This information, however, is usually proprietary, and subscription feels typically exceed $10,000 per year. Careful monitoring of periodicals and relevant books also can provide necessary background. Formal methodologies (for example, the Trend Analysis Program conducted by American Council of Life Insurance) are available to interested parties.

General trends within higher education are also important to monitor. Most readers are familiar with such information sources as NCES. Two relatively recent publications provide a great deal of general statistical information that may be useful for scenarios. These are *Three Thousand Futures*, by the Carnegie Council (1980) and *The State of the Nation and the Agenda for Higher Education*, by Howard Bowen (1982).

Especially germane to questions of student preferences and goals is the continuing examination of freshman attitudes conducted by the Cooperative Institutional Research Program of the American Council on Education. This program is carried out at the Laboratory for Research in Higher Education of the Graduate School of Education at the University of California (Los Angeles). Begun in 1966, this study is the largest continuing empirical study of American higher education. Its sample of almost 300,000 freshmen at over 500 American colleges and universities affords a wide range of biographical and demographic data, as well as information on students' career plans, educational aspirations, financial arrangements, and current attitudes. The annual data, interesting in themselves, also provide useful trend information to scenario writers in higher education.

Adoption of Premises. Having selected the elements, the scenario author must adopt premises for each. A premise is a fundamental assumption about how a particular variable will behave in a particular scenario; it defines the conduct of that variable for that scenario. Thus, if the variable under consideration were student demography, three different premises might be selected for college attendance rates. (For example, consider the different premises for college attendance characterized in the scenarios in Figure 1A and 1B.) Similar premises must be adopted for each variable included in the scenario. Figure 4 delineates possible premises for three key factors cited in Figure 3.

Figure 3. Inventory of Possible Key Factors for Scenarios

DIRECT INPUTS TO HIGHER EDUCATION

A. Funds
- -- Research
  1. Boom
  2. New Partnership
  3. Continual Decline
- -- State and Local Financial Support
  1. Enrollment-based Funding
  2. Maintain the Industry
  3. Guided Shrinkage
- -- Private Sources
  1. Continued Support
  2. Drastic Decline
- -- Student Aid
  1. Restructuring of Sources
  2. Crisis in Aid

B. Facilities
1. Replacement Schedule
2. Gradual Erosion
3. Selective Building

C. Enrollment
1. Youth Reject Schooling
2. Tooling and Retooling
3. Avocational Focus

D. Faculty
1. Brain Drain
2. Stumbling Through
3. Renewed Vigor

PROCESS FACTORS

A. Public Policy Regarding High Education
1. Market Mechanism
2. Guided Shrinkage
3. Diversity Maintained

B. Internal Academic Governance
1. Traditional Academic Values Reasserted
2. Collective Bargaining Takes Hold
3. Management Values Emerge

C. Values of Enrolled Students
1. Student Consumerism
2. Concern for the Whole Person
3. Higher Education as Low Priority

EXTERNAL FACTORS

A. Economy[a]
1. Conventional
2. Volatile
3. Decline
4. Bust

B. Computation & Communication
1. Steady Growth
2. Explosion
3. Two-Tiered Access

C. Program Demand
1. All High Tech
2. Selective Vocational Fields
3. Natural Resource Crisis
4. The Bastion of Culture

D. Societal Reaction to Higher Education
1. Greatest Asset
2. Out-of-touch
3. Selective Appreciation

E. Competition From Other Segments of Postsecondary Education
1. Little Change
2. In-House Industrial Programs
3. Proprietary Boom

F. Regulatory Climate
1. Still Greater Regulation
2. Reaganism Takes Hold

---

[a]Premises taken from *Seven Tomorrows*.

Note: Numbered items are possible premises given without explanation; see Figure 4 for detail on premises.

Figure 4. Selected Key Factors with Possible Premises for Each

ECONOMY[a]

>   Conventional - single digit inflation, slow to moderate growth
>   Volatile - sharp inflationary trends, growth followed by sharp
>   reversals
>   Decline - stagnant with slow contraction
>   Bust - mini-boom accompanied by double digit inflation followed by
>   collapse

COMPUTATION, COMMUNICATION, AND INFORMATION PROCESSING

>   Steady Growth - continual growth for both personal and professional
>   use
>   Explosion - optimistic projections are low; significant influence
>   on many aspects of life
>   Two Tier Access - only used by select segments of society; groups of
>   "have's" and "have-not's" develop

DEMAND FOR RESEARCH AND INSTRUCTIONAL PROGRAMS

>   High Tech - support for all forms of high tech remains strong but non
>   high tech fields are not seen as essential
>   Focused - emphasis is on a few select fields in the "high tech family"
>   (e.g., biogenetics)
>   Natural Resource Crisis - due to unforeseen crises in natural
>   resources, demand shifts quickly to these fields
>   Bastion of Culture - increasingly higher education is seen as
>   outmoded; the academy is seen as the "archivist of culture"

[a]Premises taken from *Seven Tomorrows.*

It is not generally understood that premise setting is the most important part of creating scenarios and requires the greatest knowledge. Once its premises are established, a scenario is set. Accordingly, premises must be based on a thorough understanding of a variable's possible behavior and must be chosen so that a scenario will be informative for its users.

To ensure that premises have credibility within an organization, local experts on important factors should be consulted. For example, the admissions and financial aid offices should be consulted about key factors dealing with financial aid or student demography. For economic variables, the treasurer, the office of institutional research, or the department of economics can be consulted. This consultation process builds ownership into the scenarios and ensures their treatment throughout the institution as serious possibilities.

Methods for Generating Scenarios. Once premises are set, two principal methods for generating scenarios are available. We shall call these methods *hard* and *soft*. Hard methods involve mathematics, models, and computers. They focus on factors that can be quantified (enrollments, budgets, research dollars). They do not include such variables as value changes. Hard methods produce scenarios of rigor and precision, which are frequently characterized in numerical ways. Soft methods, in contrast, are intuitive, involve individual personal choices, and tend to be qualitative rather than quantitative. These methods involve judgment and rely on the human mind to integrate their many variables. Examples of hard methods abound in the literature; here, we describe two salient possibilities.

The first is cross-impact analysis. A future event can be characterized individually by a mathematical probability of occurrence. Several future events, each with its own probability, interact to influence the probability, timing, and impact of each other. Cross-impact analysis affords an orderly examination of the effects of interactions among several events, using matrix algebra to examine the combinations systematically. From these results, a scenario author can improve internal consistency among a series of forecast items and challenge the basic premises of the scenario.

A more elaborate hard method of generating scenarios uses a complex computer model; its quintessential application is the world model described by Meadows and others (1972). This method, created by Jay Forrester and called system dynamics, recognizes that the general structure of a system — the many circular, interlocking, and sometimes time-delayed relationships among its components — is often just as important in determining a system's behavior as the individual components themselves are. Thus, the world model in Meadows and others (1972) employs a variety of positive feedback loops. In such loops, a chain of cause-and-effect relationships is created, such that increasing any one element in the loop will initiate a sequence of changes that will result in even more changes in the originally changed element. Time-series statistics are accumulated for each variable. When analyzed comprehensively, patterns begin to emerge, and distinct scenarios can be constructed and described.

Soft methods draw on processes of human judgment, sometimes aided by the methods of psychology and sociology. The best known of such methods is the Delphi method, developed by Olaf Helmer and others in the late 1940s and early 1950s. In the Delphi method, a panel of experts is interrogated about a number of future issues within their areas of expertise. In its classical application, the Delphi interrogation is conducted so that respondents are unknown to each other. This anonymity avoids the effects of authority, as well as the development of a consensual bandwagon. After the initial round of interrogations, the results are reported to the panel, and another round is conducted. Several rounds may be carried out in this manner. The results produced in this way can be treated statistically to yield numbers, dates, and ranges, as well as reasons for various estimates. At the end of the process, a detailed description of the issues is obtained, which shows both the central tendency of majority opinion and the range for minority disagreement. Many variants on this classic approach have been developed.

This discussion of hard and soft methods for generating scenarios inevitably raises the question of which method is better. Figure 5 compares the characteristics of the two methods; it can be seen that the methods are complementary. Thus, we believe both types of methods should be used whenever possible in scenario development.

Simply collecting data by either approach does not automatically (or even often) lead easily to distinct scenarios; scenario developers must move back and forth between the available data and their own intuitions. They must integrate their experiences and expertise with information available from their data sources. At the same time, they must understand the themes that will be most instructive and clarifying for planners using the scenarios. At this point, the process often becomes a creative intellectual struggle, as much an art as it is a science.

At this stage, too, the number of scenarios to be used must also be decided. The list of key factors and their range of specification will largely determine how many scenarios will be required for characterizing alternative futures. The greater the number of key elements, the more likely that a larger number of scenarios will be necessary. Authors writing on multiple scenario analysis disagree on the optimal number of scenarios, but most prefer fewer

Figure 5. Characteristics of Hard and Soft Methods for Scenario Development: A Comparison

HARD	SOFT
Reproducible	Not Reproducible
Strictly Logical	Intuitive
Sequential	Discontinuous
Quantitative	Descriptive
Data-Dependent	Not Necessarily Numerical
Constrained by Model	Not Limited by Constraints

than five, simply because it is difficult for users to remember important differences when there are many possibilities to consider. Therefore, some authors even conclude that two or three is the ideal number. Others argue that three, or any other odd number is not a desirable number, because the tendency will be to select the middle scenario. Still others argue that two is too small a number, because one scenario typically is selected as good and the other as bad, and the important objective of introducing uncertainty into the planning process is removed. To decide on the number of scenarios, authors must determine which key factors provide the critical differences to alternative futures. This process will present a picture of organizational structure from which the number of possible scenarios will become intuitively obvious.

Producing the Scenarios. Once the variables are chosen, the premises set, and the themes of each scenario agreed upon, scenario writing itself can begin. For detailed scenarios, the future events that lead to them should be specified. In writing scenarios, it is important to understand the distinction between events, on the one hand, and trends, on the other. Both must be employed in scenario construction, and each plays a different role. An event is an expected or unexpected discontinuity, and it generally has a defined time limit and frequently is followed by a change in the trends of interest. Examples of past events include establishment of the Basic Educational Opportunity Grant program in the 1960s and the anti–Vietnam war protests in the early 1970s. A trend, in contrast, is a course of direction of events. It generally lacks a defined time limit and can best be described by a time series or some other continuing indicator. Examples of trends are rising or falling birthrates, high school graduation rates, and minority enrollment in higher education. Plausible scenarios encompass trends as well as events of significance.

A format for presenting scenarios must also be selected. As one example, Shell Oil Company describes each of its two scenarios in a brief paragraph at the beginning of its seventy-page scenario report. The remaining pages contain graphs and tables projecting external factors critical for planning. Each graph or table contains two projections, one for each scenario. Obviously, this example is highly tabular, with only minimal text. In contrast, *Seven Tomorrows* (Hawken and others, 1982) presents seven scenarios for the future of the United States between 1980 and the year 2000. Each scenario is a twenty-page essay, artfully written from the imaginary perspective of a person in the year 2000. Two tables presented with each scenario summarize major social indicators for the year 2000.

Obviously, the choice of hard versus soft scenario methodology will heavily influence the format, but the results of a hard methodology can be presented with text alone. The selection of a format should be dictated largely by the accepted learning styles of scenario users. If people in an organization are accustomed to working only with brief memos and tabular data, then the format of the scenario should recognize this style; in higher education planning, text supplemented with a few tables or charts would be appropriate.

Zentner's (1975, 1978, 1982) experience in industry demonstrates that the most effective approach to scenario writing is a group effort. The best groups are often interdisciplinary, and so hard method results can be blended with results from soft methods. Advocates of each method are given an arena for confrontation and collaboration.

Responsibility for Scenarios. In this discussion, we have frequently referred to the scenario draftsman. This person should come from the central planning staff, where the overall needs of the organization are perceived and addressed, and where environmental forces — including funds, demographics, curriculum requirements, and legislative factors — are tracked. We do not imply that the planning staff should have sole responsibility for scenario development; faculty members and staff members should be tapped for information and ideas. Ultimately, however, scenario drafting and coordination are probably best left with the planning staff, for the reasons mentioned above.

In universities, planning is frequently a function of presidents or chancellors. In colleges, planning is a task of deans. For scenarios to be used effectively at different levels of institutions, they should be developed and distributed with the understanding and support of the university officer holding ultimate planning responsibility.

Why Use Scenarios?

Let us now discuss more fully why multiple scenario analysis (MSA) is potentially useful for higher education planning. As pointed out, the underlying premise of MSA is that the future has been and always will be unpredictable. MSA is potentially a powerful technique because it not only recognizes this fundamental characteristic of the future but also builds on it. Although detailed treatments of a single future can be useful background information for strategic planners, it would be shortsighted for colleges or universities to construct plans around a single view of the future. Decision makers may prefer the enrollment projections of Carol Frances (1980), Stephen Dresch (1975), the Carnegie Council (1980), or their own versions. In any event, wise decision makers position their institutions for reaction to unpredictable series of unfolding events. Scenario use is not a panacea, but it does bring uncertainty to the forefront of the planning process.

As a wider range of possibilities is considered, a wider set of values is also incorporated into planning. MSA forces planners to put aside single perspectives dictated by personally held values and to consider the possibility of other futures predicated on other value sets.

Since planning has tended historically to rely on the analysis of changing trends projected to continue in a smooth curve (even though the direction of this curve may change), it is necessary to recognize now that significant change often coalesces around discrete events, not around the smooth progression of a trend. By examining possible events with potentially serious consequences, as with multiple scenarios, institutions will be better prepared for the future.

Grappling with different scenarios also raises consciousness about the cause-and-effect relationship of selected events and trends in the environment. This is pointed out by Enzer: "The glue that holds [these] scenarios together is a mixture of probability and causality, or simply plausibility. Causality suggests that current trends and conditions contain the harbingers of tomorrow's changes, and that tomorrow's changes are the monitoring signals of subsequent changes, and so on. To be effective for strategic planning, a scenario must be sufficiently detailed to trace the causality chain from the present to the new future state—it must be 'explicitly plausible'" (1981, p. 471).

Presenting effective scenarios, regardless of their format or length, requires integrative thinking. Rather than examining only a single factor, such as enrollment projections, authors and users of scenarios are forced to examine the interplay of many factors. Quantitative and qualitative data alike can be incorporated into the analysis. This methodology is not constraining or limiting. The complex of factors under consideration is too great for either a stochastic model or a multiple regression equation. Thus, the process gives a primary role to the most useful and most underused factor in the planning process, human judgment.

Scenarios also provide a useful context for discussions of planning. When each scenario is given a different title, a useful vocabulary is provided for a variety of discussions. In this way, scenarios give people within an institution a shared frame of reference for the future.

One potential drawback of scenarios is the time and effort required to construct them. Corporations that use them usually have centralized planning staffs responsible for generating background materials and coordinating the planning process. Typically, higher education institutions have only skeletal staffs to handle all these responsibilities, but an office of institutional research could generate three or four plausible scenarios for inclusion with planning instruction.

Scenario development must be rigorous and analytical. Hastily constructed, internally inconsistent scenarios will not be accepted. Statistical data supporting the scenario's plausibility are nearly indispensable. But scenario development is not solely a matter of methodology. Indeed, the methodology serves only as the tool of the developers.

Most important for scenario draftsmen is understanding the use to which scenarios will be put as well as how elements of scenarios affect their use.

Figure 6. Good and Bad Scenarios: Some Criteria

Good	Bad
Intelligible	Hard to understand
Useful	Difficult to use
Interesting	Dull
Provides data required for addressing key issues	Lacks relevant data
Plausible	Presents trends and events which are hard to believe or inconsistent
Relevant to planner's needs	Little information related to planning

Scenario effectiveness depends on how scenarios speak to policy makers and planners and on how they respond. Unless draftsmen perceive the nature of that dialogue, scenarios will miss their mark and lack relevance. For those reasons, scenario draftsmen must begin their task with a clear understanding of institutional needs. Throughout the development process, those needs must be kept constantly in mind. The result of understanding and intelligent methodology will be scenarios that can make substantial contributions to planners, policy makers, and ultimately to higher education.

References

Bowen, H. *The State of the Nation and the Agenda for Higher Education.* San Francisco: Jossey-Bass, 1982.

Carnegie Council on Policy Studies in Higher Education. *Three Thousand Futures.* San Francisco: Jossey-Bass, 1980.

Cornish, E. *The Study of the Future.* Washington, D.C.: World Future Society, 1977.

Dresch, S. P. "Demography, Technology, and Higher Education: Toward a Formal Model of Education Adaptation." *Journal of Political Economy,* 1975, *83,* 535–569.

Enzer, S. "Exploring Long-Term Business Climates and Strategies with INTERAX." *Futures,* 1981, *13,* 468-482.

Frances, C. *College Enrollment Trends: Testing the Conventional Wisdom Against the Facts.* Washington, D.C.: American Council on Education, 1980.

68

Hawken, P., Ogilvy, J., and Schwartz, P. *Seven Tomorrows.* New York: Bantam, 1982.

Kahn, H., and Wiener, A. J. *The Year 2000.* New York: Macmillan, 1967.

Meadows, D. H., Meadows, D. L., Randers, J., and Behrens, W. W., III. *The Limits to Growth: A Report for the Club of Rome's Project on the Predicament of Mankind.* New York: Universe Books, 1972.

Wilson, I. H. "Sociopolitical Forecasting: A New Dimension to Strategic Planning." *Michigan Business Review,* July 1974, p. 15.

Zentner, R. D. "Scenarios in Forecasting." *Chemical and Engineering News,* October 6, 1975, 22–34.

Zentner, R. D. "Development of Scenarios: An Overview." Paper presented at the annual meeting of the North American Society for Corporate Planning, 1978.

Zentner, R. D. "Scenarios Past, Present, and Future." *Long Range Planning,* 1982, *15,* 12–20.

Richard B. Heydinger is assistant to the vice-president for academic affairs at the University of Minnesota. He was also selected as a Kellogg National Fellow to study strategic planning and the future of higher education.

Rene D. Zentner is associate dean of the University of Houston Law Center. He was formerly associated with E. I. Du Pont de Nemours & Company, Inc., Tracerlab, Inc., and Shell Oil Company.

Understanding the link between futures research and strategic planning
is crucial to effective long-range policy planning and administration.
So too is understanding current trends and the latest developments
in the methodology of futures research. This chapter focuses on
both subjects.

New Directions in
Futures Methodology

Selwyn Enzer

In discussing new directions in futures research methodology, it is useful to review the situation that led to the establishment of futures research as a discipline, the impact the discipline has had on our ability to manage the future, and the current situation with regard to priority research needs. The beginnings of futures research can be traced to the military planning that followed World War II. To avoid military obsolescence, it was deemed necessary for our nation to be the first to develop key technologies. This goal placed a high premium on technological forecasting (TF), an activity that attempts to predict the future, but with probabilities attached. The success of TF in guiding military planning led to its use by other planners as the pace of change quickened.

In the mid- to late 1960s, strategic planners came to view TF as a possible way of gaining a better understanding of the changing social environment. Nevertheless, the nature of the uncertainty surrounding business and social environments was so much greater than that encountered in TF that the value of describing possible future conditions, with probabilities attached, was questionable: Whereas technological forecasters could rely on what they called the "technical imperative" as a guarantee that any technically sound development would be pursued, societal forecasting had no comparable paradigm. The futures research community, which was just emerging at this time, did

J. L. Morrison, W. L. Renfro, and W. I. Boucher (Eds.). *Applying Methods and Techniques of Futures Research.*
New Directions for Institutional Research, no. 39. San Francisco: Jossey-Bass, September 1983.

not fully recognize the dichotomy between what strategic planners were seeklñg and the kinds of insight that actually could be produced. Futures researchers presumed that a comprehensive description of alternatives would enable strategic planners to deal more effectively with the changing environment. The strategic planners, in contrast, were expecting better predictions about future changes; this, after all, was what TF did for military planners.

That dichotomy is only now being addressed by futures researchers through alternative scenarios and analytic procedures that combine forecasts with strategic planning. These procedures encourage planners to develop robust strategies to perform effectively over the full range of uncertainty that is likely to be encountered. The development of methods combining futures research with strategic planning and describing the consequences of these considerations for the entire organization is likely to dominate in the years to come.

The Emergence of Futures Research

A study conducted toward the end of World War II by the president's scientific advisory group, headed by Dr. Theodore Von Karman, contributed strongly to futures research as a distinct discipline. This study, commissioned for the Army Air Corps by General Hap Arnold, involved a forecast of scientific developments that might be realized over the next twenty years and that might significantly change the nature of warfare and, hence, military strategy. The purpose of the forecast was to identify priority research activities that would prevent the Air Corps from falling behind in military capability in the future.

This study resulted in a brilliant report, *Towards New Horizons* (Von Karman, 1945). Because the report was classified as secret, it was not widely disseminated, but it was extremely important, not only in guiding the research program carried out by the Air Force in the 1950s and the 1960s but also in helping to promote the political consensus needed to secure funding for the program. In futures research jargon, one of the unintended, indirect consequences of the study was to improve the efficiency with which the arms race could be conducted. In retrospect, we can note that this early futures research activity's ability to affect strategic decisions appears to have been greater than that of all the futures research activities that followed.

What was it about Von Karman's work that made it a futures research study, as opposed to any other type of study, and why was it able to guide strategic decisions? Clearly, one reason for its success was the outstanding credentials of the research team members, but the main reason was that its forecasts were based on the technical imperative, which, again, assumed that any technology offering a potentially high payoff in military improvement would be pursued. Since the decision makers agreed with this assumption, they pursued the recommendations made by the scientific forecasters, and since the technical quality of the results was outstanding, their actions turned these forecasts into tomorrow's realities. The early success of TF largely resulted from the workings of self-fulfilling prophecy.

But why do we classify this effort today as a futures research study? Basically, we do this because its findings were almost exclusively based on judgments about the future and because these judgments were used to develop complex scenarios, as opposed to identifying only the next generation of military-related breakthroughs, although the study team members did do an excellent job of anticipating major future developments. While they neither identified the possibility of developing the transistor nor anticipated any comparable developments, they did anticipate the dawn of the guided-missile era and described the new military situation that missiles and nuclear weapons would create. Finally, the research programs suggested by this team appropriately positioned the United States for capitalizing on those systems made possible by the invention of the transistor, even though the transistor itself was missed in the forecast.

Indirectly, the Von Karman study also contributed strongly to the popularity of TF in military circles. This development occurred because the research programs adopted as a result of the study created an environment that emphasized the need to do long-range forecasting. As a result, many TF activities were carried out by aerospace planners long before TF was fashionable. Indeed, the extent of TF's popularity and the rich variety of methods developed for conducting TF were largely unknown until they were discovered by Erich Jantsch in 1967. Jantsch's research report on technological forecasting (Jantsch, 1967) put these isolated ideas about forecasting into an analytical framework, which — when combined with ideas presented in Kahn and Wiener's *The Year 2000* (1967), de Jouvenel's *The Art of Conjecture* (1967), Dennis Gabor's *Inventing the Future* (1964), and several other works — led to the recognition that a new discipline had been born.

The thrust of this new discipline was to expand traditional sources of information about the future — data and trends about the past — by including subjective information about the future itself. Not surprisingly, therefore, early futures research efforts focused almost exclusively on the development of methods for capturing and synthesizing informed judgment about future changes.

This process led to the development and use of such methods as the Delphi technique, scenario writing, brainstorming, cross-impact analysis, relevance analysis, trend-impact analysis, KSIM (a variation on cross-impact analysis), and system dynamics for applying informed judgment to the exploration of long-term future change. Many of these methods were not developed exclusively for forecasting applications; for example, Delphi was primarily developed to elicit judgmental inputs for model building and goal formulation, but its subsequent use as a method for forecasting possible future events, including their likelihood, timing, and impacts, has caused this method to dominate the research.

Scenario writing was originally used to describe plausible sequences of developments leading to particular situations that planners and analysts regarded as strategically important. Analysts did not necessarily claim that their scenarios were very likely or even that sequences presented in scenarios were the only way that future situations could arise. Since its origins, scenario writing has come to be used for more grandiose strategic purposes than merely describing one way in which a different strategic environment can emerge.

Cross-impact analysis was originally developed to improve the accuracy of Delphi forecasts (Gordon, 1968; Gordon and Hayward, 1968). The hypothesis was that a weakness of judgmental forecasting was failure to take into account all the indirect impacts of other changes on the events or situations being forecast. Notwithstanding the possible validity of this hypothesis, early cross-impact models based on this assumption proved to be operationally sound because these models — which modified probability estimates by including the indirect effects — could not handle situations in which people providing judgments did recognize indirect impacts. Cross-impact analysis was later developed as a method for combining the results of interdependent forecasts about events and trends so as to generate alternative plausible future scenarios (Enzer, 1977).

Priorities in futures research lie now in implementation, that is, in improving the relevance of research to strategic planning and decision making. The naive futures research assumption — that if better information about the future were available, more farsighted decisions would automatically follow — has been thoroughly discredited. The current priority for futures research is to make futures research information more relevant to the strategic choices that are open to public and private organizations. The thrust of this research is toward analytical procedures integrating strategic analysis with alternative futures in ways that clearly elaborate the importance of change to the user's organization.

Methodological research often starts out in one direction and is revised to address some new consideration as new insight is achieved; we might expect the same to occur as futures research methodology seeks new directions in the years to come. Since these new directions are likely to focus on the strategic implementation of futures research findings, it is important to review the nature of the strategic problem and to assess the changes that have taken place in strategic planning since the emergence of futures research.

The Impact of Futures Research on Strategic Planning

During the past several decades, institutions increasingly have recognized the inadequacy of strategic plans based on the assumption that trend projections over the next twenty years would be extensions of the past twenty years. As a result, futures research methods have focused on anticipating future changes and developing alternative scenarios. Initially, these images came from individual research—Toffler's *Future Shock* (1970) and Kahn's *Thinking the Unthinkable* (1962) and *The Next Two Hundred Years* (1976)—but soon the new futures research organizations were also contributing their own products, including The Institute for the Future's *Future of Employee Benefits* (Gordon, 1969) and *Issues and Opportunities in the State of Connecticut* (Enzer and DeBrigard, 1969). Subsequently, government and private organizations pursued scenario development projects on their own. The Trend Analysis Reports (TAP) produced by the American Council of Life Insurance, the Office of Technology Assessment, and Shell's multiple scenario approach are but a few examples of the degree to which organizations have internalized their futures research activities.

The popular business magazines soon picked up on the appeal of long-range scenarios. *Fortune, Business Week, Time, U.S. News & World Report*, and *Newsweek* new regularly run features on long-term change. There are almost no institutions that use a single set of assumptions, as opposed to multiple scenarios, in their strategic planning. Nevertheless, few institutions have developed procedures for using a range of alternatives to develop more robust strategies, strategies that can respond to many possible future environments without incurring severe losses. Indeed, very few organizations even stress the importance of robust strategies. Correcting this imbalance is likely to be the primary thrust of methodological developments in futures research over the next two decades. Procedures are needed that not only explore alternative futures but also integrate these alternatives with strategic planning to develop robust, long-term corporate plans and monitoring systems.

Needed: An Improved Image of Alternative Futures

Since futures research is concerned with the study of alternative futures, not with predicting what will occur, it has confused both laypeople and strategic planners. The popular conception is that futures research predicts the conditions that will occur at some later time—the "future present." The futures researchers' view, however, is that the future is inherently uncertain, and that the important task is to determine both what "future presents" are possible and the best strategies for coping with these possibilities. In short, forecasters are concerned with what will happen, while futures researchers are concerned with the process that is capable of creating the alternative futures.

Metaphorically, alternative futures can be viewed as possible outcomes that may follow from the toss of a pair of "fair" dice. Futures researchers are concerned with anticipating the various faces that may appear on the dice and with estimating the probability of each possibility, while forecasters are concerned with predicting the outcome. Strategists deal with how organizational resources should be allocated to take advantage of (or merely survive) changes that may occur over the long term; they would rather ponder a single future than many possibilities. Science can go no farther than describing the process; this process produces the probabilities of the various outcomes. The pseudo-science of futures research is similarly limited: In other words, while futures research may use semiscientific methods to elaborate on possible outcomes and their respective probabilities, it does not reduce the uncertainty associated with future possibilities. In fact, it generally increases the perceived number of possibilities and, hence, the strategic uncertainty. Strategic planners often view this result as counterproductive, since they really would like to know what the "future present" will be, so that they can design strategies to take full advantage of its opportunities and avoid its pitfalls. If only it were so simple!

Uncertainty about the future is a function neither of the forecaster nor of his crystal ball, but of conditions surrounding the forecast. A strategist attempting to decide how to posture an organization must recognize both the uncertainty of the environment and the potential need to deal with any of the possibilities this environment can produce; it is not sufficient to bank exclusively on the most likely outcome. But how do we design robust strategies?

The first step is to understand fully the uncertainty concerning alternative futures. This, in turn, requires understanding the process of how a single present emerges from many possible futures. A generally shared model for this process is as follows: *The present is a continuation of existing trends, subject to modification by uncertain changes and the exercise of human choice.* Uncertain changes involve technological developments, natural phenomena, accidents, and other conditions over which organizations have limited or no control. The uncertainty surrounding such changes cannot be eliminated by forecasting; it is a result of the environment itself, of our incomplete understanding of how the environment changes, or of some combination of both factors. So long as uncertain changes can affect some critical aspect of a future condition, the future cannot be predicted precisely. If the uncertain future changes can be anticipated, however, the alternative futures they suggest can be evaluated judgmentally. Such anticipation will not reveal unknown, unthought-of possibilities, though; these will always elude judgmental processes, but a process that systematically calls for thinking about possible unlikely future changes can reduce the number of unanticipated possibilities to the smallest possible set.

So, continuing trends and uncertain changes together do not completely describe the alternative possibilities. It is also necessary to consider the policy changes that organizations may introduce in the future. Policy changes are like uncertain changes except that the uncertainty surrounding policy changes derives not from incomplete understanding but rather from human uncertainty regarding future decisions. Decision uncertainty is a true uncertainty, in that human choice is not always predictable (even though it may be understandable), and policy changes are a result of human choice. Unlike, for example, the atom—which, when its secrets were revealed, continued to behave as it had before—exposure of a corporate decision rule often leads to revision of the rule. Finally, policy changes are rarely independent of the contexts in which they are made.

In summary, a single present emerges from a set of alternative futures via a cybernetic process, in which evolving conditions are periodically affected by uncertain changes. The revised conditions are evaluated by social organizations to determine or change policy choices; in turn, these change the evolving conditions and set the stage for the next cycle.

The Dichotomy Between Futures Research and Strategic Planning

The fundamental assumption of futures research is that society is not predestined or otherwise constrained to a particular long-run end state. With such an assumption, soothsaying is simply not possible. The future is likely to be significantly different from the present in many important ways. Futures research is concerned with understanding long-term social conditions, their prospects for change, and the direct and indirect consequences of these changes—where society is heading and the degree to which this destination can be altered. Futures research is also concerned with understanding how various social groups (stakeholders) concerned about the evolving conditions may assess alternative futures. The objective of studying alternative social conditions is to gain an understanding of where these conditions are likely to lead, where they can lead, and where different stakeholders think they should lead.

Strategic planning concerns itself with managing mission-oriented social organizations. It is inherently value-oriented, setting objectives and goals with an eye to pursuing its mission and allocating its resources and management talents to achieve those goals. Futures research is primarily concerned with the social environments in which organizational strategies are to be carried out. For strategic planners, the social environment is the organization's external environment. Information about the external environment is essential at all levels of corporate planning. It is needed to decide on changes in organizational mission, to establish strategic objectives, to explore alternative long-range directions, and to decide what should be done in the short run. With or without futures research, strategic planning must be based on some insight into or assumption about the direction of the external environment.

Traditional strategic planning exhibits two important structural weaknesses in its handling of long-term change: It generally assumes a complete separation between the organization and the external environment—that is, that the organization cannot and does not affect social conditions—and it is also liable to underestimate the external environment's variability. In many cases, strategic planning actually requires a single set of assumptions about the future. This forces organizations to act as if the future were predictable, even though planners and decision makers realize the fallacy of that assumption. Organizations whose strategic planning ignores uncertainties in the external environment ultimately ignore their own plans. In such organizations, formal strategic planning is purely cosmetic, and real strategic planning is carried out by management acting in an entrepreneurial manner.

This circumstance highlights an important issue that futures researchers overlooked for many years, namely, that organizations that use alternative futures effectively often have to change how they handle uncertainty at the strategic planning stage. Futures researchers used to pursue their analyses with the implicit assumption that a better understanding of future uncertainty would automatically lead to more effective strategic plans. Strategic planners, in contrast, generally were looking for more accurate predictions of what future conditions would be like. Every strategic planner knew how to use increasingly accurate predictions, but few were able to cope with a range of alternatives. As a result, even after it became commonplace for corporations to develop several alternative scenarios for strategic planning, actual planning procedures often could address only one scenario. In such cases, the scenario thought to be most likely was used as the single assumption in an obsolete strategic planning process, and the impact of alternative scenarios on organizational strategy was all but eliminated.

Futures Research and Strategic Planning as Integrated Activities

The first procedure for integrating futures research forecasting with strategic decision making was demonstrated at a seminar for public administrators in Bruges, Belgium, in 1970 (Enzer, 1970). The demonstration consisted of a two-day workshop, during which participants explored alternative futures for Europe and evaluated alternative strategies that could be pursued to control the outcomes. In this workshop, participants developed a cross-impact model of possible future changes for Europe over a ten-year period. Next, they tried to develop alternative strategies for managing anticipated changes in ways that they considered most effective. The cross-impact model was then used in a simulation to generate a range of scenarios against which the various strategies were tested.

This procedure was used in a later series of workshops in the United

States and Canada to demonstrate its ability to explore alternative futures reflecting combined strategies that might be adopted by different organizations (Enzer, Boucher, and Lazar, 1971; Enzer, 1971). These workshops also included assessments of the desirability, from different stakeholder perspectives, of various outcomes.

The analytical research that followed these early workshops proceeded in two directions. One emphasized the benefits of developing and using inexpensive ("quick and dirty") procedures for identifying and exploring macro strategic alternatives. The other attempted more detailed analysis of the alternative scenarios in ways that permitted them to be linked to organizational planning models. Typical of the inexpensive approaches are Focused Planning (Boucher, 1972) and QUEST (Nanus, 1982); typical of the more detailed approaches are KSIM (Kane, 1972) and INTERAX (Enzer, 1980).

Quick Environmental Scanning Technique (QUEST)

QUEST is a procedure designed to help top executives and planners keep abreast of the rapid pace of change and its implications for organizational strategy. This procedure produces (1) a broad and comprehensive first statement of a futures research analysis of the external environment and (2) an assessment of an organization's strategic options for handling the environment. QUEST draws on the information about the changing environment already known to organizational managers. QUEST provides a quick, inexpensive way to share this information systematically and focus managers' attention on areas that can benefit from more detailed planning.

A QUEST exercise in an organization generally begins with a manager's or a planner's recognition of some potentially critical strategic problem. The activity requires management support, a QUEST moderator, and nominal clerical work. The moderator's role is crucial to success. In some situations, it may be most effective to use an outside consultant as a moderator. An outside moderator can facilitate the inquiry, including preparation of reports, without eliminating the need for a project coordinator who is also a member of the organization. Being from outside the organization allows the moderator to ask questions that challenge obsolete management positions and to maintain an even-handed perspective on ideas generated in the course of the activity. Nevertheless, translating the results of QUEST sessions into scenarios that address strategic problems in ways that reflect an understanding of the corporate culture requires familiarity with the organization, and the inside project coordinator must provide this perspective.

QUEST involves four steps, including two planning sessions, and can easily be completed within one month. The first step is to prepare for the activity. This step involves four tasks: precisely defining the strategic issue to be analyzed, selecting a group of from twelve to fifteen participants, preparing a notebook that contains pertinent and readily available information, and selecting suitable dates and distraction-free sites for the QUEST workshops.

The notebook serves two purposes: It elaborates on the issue and it expedites the workshop by eliminating the need for participants to rehash the general wisdom. (Some researchers, however, avoid the introduction of already existing material into strategic planning sessions, on the grounds that such material may restrict participants' thinking.)

The second step is to carry out the first planning session. This step usually takes place in an all-day workshop in which participants are encouraged to think about the strategic environment in the broadest possible terms. To ensure the relevance of these deliberations, the session begins with discussion of the strategic issue's context. This discussion includes developing statements of the organization's strategic mission and of the purposes and objectives reflected in the mission, as well as identifying the key stakeholder groups (both from within and outside the organization) and determining their respective priorities. The discussion then shifts to identifying changes (critical events and shifts in trends) that may have significant impacts on some aspect of the external environment. The remainder of this session is spent evaluating the likelihood and magnitude of these changes, as well as their cross-impacts on each other and on the organization's strategic posture.

During this open-ended investigation, participants are encouraged to think broadly and comprehensively of important strategic changes, even those considered to be very unlikely, but at this time they are not permitted to discuss strategic implications of these changes. This constraint derives directly from Delphi and brainstorming experience, in which evaluations and responses are always delayed until a complete slate of alternatives has been developed.

The third step is to summarize the results of the workshop in a brief written report. This summary is generally divided into two parts: assessment of the organization's strategic position, mission, objectives, stakeholders, and so forth; and a statement of alternative scenarios describing the external environments the organization may face over the strategic period.

It is essential that the ideas presented in this report be attributed to the group as a whole, not to individual participants. For the evaluation to be effective, it is important for the group to consider each idea on the basis of its merit, not its pedigree. Time for reflection is provided, since the report on the first meeting is distributed to participants a few days before the second meeting, at which strategic options are explored.

The final step in QUEST is to hold a strategy meeting, usually for four hours. In this meeting the report is reviewed and the strategic options facing the organization are identified. These options are evaluated by the group for responsiveness to the evolving external environment and for consistency with organizational strengths and weaknesses. QUEST is not expected to produce any immediate change in strategy; after all, it is just a first statement of a strategic review. What should result from QUEST is a series of precise assignments designed to evaluate the most important options in greater depth. Each of these assignments should describe briefly the general nature of the inquiry needed to evaluate each option properly and should specify a completion date. Assignments should be made during this final session and subsequently confirmed in writing by the manager who sponsored the activity.

INTERAX

INTERAX is used for in-depth analysis of a strategic issue. An INTERAX analysis is normally preceded by a QUEST-like activity. INTERAX can be most effective when used in the context of strategic management — that is, management of a long-term issue that is expected to change over time. Such issues cannot be fully resolved at the time the analysis is conducted and require frequent updating.

INTERAX is a process for generating plausible alternative futures by using computer models and human analysts in an interactive simulation. Each INTERAX simulation produces a single possible scenario. When used in strategic planning, INTERAX generates scenarios of the external environment and of organizational performance simultaneously. The INTERAX simulation may be stopped after each projected year. During these pauses, intermediate conditions can be reviewed and policies changed. Any intermediate policy changes are kept in force until the simulation is completed. When the next simulation begins, all inputs are returned to their nominal settings.

To generate an INTERAX scenario, two sets of inputs must be loaded into the computer programs. The first set consists of nominal trend projections, including forecasts of the organization's performance over time and the exogenous trend forecasts on which the performance projections are based. These projections are referred to as the nominal forecast conditions. The nominal forecast is not explicitly loaded into the model, but it is based on an assumed organizational strategy (herein referred to as the nominal strategy). Organizational performance projections may be in the form of a model — a system dynamics model, a corporate simulator, or some other analytical framework. An organizational model increases the system's flexibility for testing and evaluating alternative strategies, but such a model is not essential. It is important to note that INTERAX does not generate the nominal forecast; the nominal forecast is part of the input to the simulation. The second set of inputs required for the INTERAX simulation consists of a cross-impact model, including descriptions of events whose occurrence would have important consequences for organizational strategy; in other words, the occurrence of these events would affect either the exogenous projections on which the nominal forecast is based or the implicit assumptions on which the strategy is based. For example, if the nominal forecast is based on a 10 percent inflation rate over the next ten years, any change in this exogenous variable would produce a corresponding change in some portion of the nominal forecast. A change in an implicit assumption could result from a tax-code revision that affects the internal calculations on which the nominal forecast is based.

INTERAX uses these inputs — the nominal trend projections and the cross-impact model, with the associated elements — in a simulation that proceeds as follows:

- The time period is divided into annual intervals.
- The cross-impact model computes the probabilities of occurrence for each of the events in the first year.
- A random number simulation is used to decide which if any of the events occurred in the first year.
- The results of the simulated first year are used to adjust the probabilities of the remaining events in subsequent years and the exogenous trend forecasts for the end of the first year and to change their projected values for subsequent years.
- The adjusted exogenous trend forecasts are used to revise the organization's performance for the end of the first year and its projected performance for the subsequent years.
- The computer reports these results to the participants interacting with the simulation and then stops, awaiting additional instructions.
- The participating analysts assume that the simulated time is the real time — that is now one year later — and assess the result as they think they would have if this outcome had actually taken place. They decide which aspects of their strategy (if any) they would change. These changes are appended to the computer models, and the next year's results are simulated, using the same procedure described for the first year.
- The simulation repeats these steps until all the years in the strategic time period have been covered.

With the completion of all the intervals, one possible long-term future is described. The description of this future consists of the trend projections over time, the events that occurred and the years in which they occurred, a narrative (usually taped) describing how the policy analysts viewed the simulated conditions, and the policy changes introduced by the analysts and the impacts of these changes on the resulting scenario. The policy analysts may decide that the scenario that has just been developed was good, bad, or mediocre. They may wish to try another run, but in any subsequent run the probabilistic changes may work out differently; for example, scientific breakthroughs that occurred before may not occur this time. Hence, while repeated simulations may provide increasingly better understanding of strategic options for dealing with possible alternative futures, the simulation does not provide any pat answers; policy analysts will always face the same uncertainty when starting a new simulation.

Simulations in which policy analysts attempt to manage long-term strategies under constant uncertainty are very similar to situations faced in the real world. The benefit of simulations is that they help the analysts to appreciate uncertainty in the environment and to devise strategies robust enough to cope with uncertainty. Simulations also provide an understanding of the kinds of follow-up actions that can be taken after initial choices have been made, and they help analysts identify conditions to be monitored for early warning of pending changes.

By repeating a simulation many times and with different groups of simulators, it is possible to develop a rich appreciation of alternative futures likely to be encountered. This procedure can minimize surprise when the transition is made from the analytical model to the real world. Furthermore, the increased foresight produced by simulations is not restricted to the executive levels of the organization; through coupling of scenarios to models describing the full spectrum of organizational functions, alternative scenarios can be related to all pertinent organizational activities — costs, income, development, performance, personnel, and capital facilities, for example.

Perhaps the most important contribution that INTERAX can make to improving strategic planning is in its continued use, over the years, as strategies are implemented. The pattern of uncertainty captured in the initial INTERAX model will be subject to change as anticipations give way to reality. These changes may in turn suggest revisions to organizational strategy, but the effort required to revise the INTERAX data and update strategic plans is only a fraction of the effort required to establish the initial data base.

Strategy Rooms

There is a strong similarity between the strategic management of an organization and the strategic activities of military field commanders (not to be confused with military planners). Field commanders attempt to assess their strategic positions in just the same way that futures researchers advise strategic planners to assess their positions. Field commanders try to understand all the possible situations they may face during battle, deciding on strategies believed to be satisfactory (optimal) and sufficiently robust to respond to alternative situations, should they occur, and simultaneously implementing selected strategies and making preparations for revising them. In preparing for change, field commanders identify enemy movements to be expected in the event of change, post sentries to watch for such movements, and quickly revise strategies in the event that sentries detect unanticipated enemy movements.

On a somewhat slower time scale, strategic planners are called upon to perform analogous tasks. They, too, must anticipate strategic changes in the environment, select strategies that are not only likely to succeed but also responsive to these changes, identify the warning signs of change in the environment, post sentries to monitor those warning signs, and be prepared to modify strategies and respond to new conditions.

To give field commanders prebattle experience of combat uncertainty, military planners have devised war games. War games simulate informational aspects of combat conditions as closely as possible. The objectives of war games is to help field commanders perfect their judgment and timing prior to battle. These simulations are generally carried out in war rooms.

It is only natural for analogous strategic simulations to be pursued in organizations that are exposed to rapidly changing conditions. These activities can be conducted in places called strategy rooms. Research into strategy rooms (or decision rooms) is still in its infancy, and so it is still difficult to describe what their characteristics ought to be like. Clearly, they should be able to facilitate QUEST and INTERAX analyses, which means that they should provide access to the latest and most accurate information relevant to the strategic issue under investigation. Strategy rooms should also provide the methodological support that participants need for evaluating the alternatives suggested by this information. The whole point of any strategy room is to make all the implications of this information relevant to strategic alternatives facing the organization, so that participants can test their judgment in situations closely resembling the possibilities they may encounter in the real world. The design of a strategy room involves more than merely packaging the best information and analytical capabilities into one place; it also involves designing information systems that are sufficiently user-friendly to assist in the understanding of alternative conditions and in the synthesis of alternative strategies. The data bases, simulation models, and analytical procedures needed for implementing initial versions of strategy rooms already exist. Once in place, these facilities will very likely be used for exploring alternatives and for management training, as well as for developing and testing alternative strategies. These human–machine facilities are likely to show us the next steps toward developing the farsighted manager who was envisioned by the futures research community when it first came into being.

References

Boucher, W. I. *Report on a Hypothetical Focused Planning Effort (FPE)*. Glastonbury, Conn.: The Futures Group, 1972.

deJouvenel, B. *The Art of Conjecture*. New York: Basic Books, 1967.

Enzer, S. "A Case Study Using Forecasting as a Decision-Making Aid." *Futures,* 1970, *2* (4), 341–362.

Enzer, S. *Federal/State Science Policy and Connecticut.* Menlo Park, Calif.: Institute for the Future, 1971.

Enzer, S. "Cross Impact Methods in Assessing Long-Term Oceanographic Changes." In P. D. Wilmot and A. Slingerland (Eds.), *Technology Assessment and the Oceans.* Boulder, Colo.: Westview Press, 1977.

Enzer, S. "INTERAX — An Interactive Model for Studying Future Business Environments: Parts I and II." *Technological Forecasting and Social Change,* 1980, *17* (2-3), 141–159, 211–242.

Enzer, S., and DeBrigard, R. *Issues and Opportunities in the State of Connecticut.* Menlo Park, Calif.: Institute for the Future, 1969.

Enzer, S., Boucher, W. I., and Lazar, F. D. *Futures Research as an Aid to Government Planning in Canada.* Menlo Park, Calif.: Institute for the Future, 1971.

Gabor, D. *Inventing the Future.* New York: Knopf, 1964.

Gordon, T. J. "New Approaches to Delphi." In J. R. Bright (Ed.), *Technological Forecasting for Industry and Government.* Englewood Cliffs, N.J.: Prentice Hall, 1968.

Gordon, T. J. *Future of Employee Benefits.* Vols. 1-4. Menlo Park, Calif.: Institute for the Future, 1969.

Gordon, T. J., and Hayward, J. "Initial Experiments with the Cross-Impact Matrix Method of Forecasting." *Futures,* 1968, *1* (2), 100–116.

Jantsch, E. *Technological Forecasting in Perspective.* Paris: Organization for Economic Cooperation and Development, 1967.

Kahn, H. *Thinking about the Unthinkable.* New York: Horizon Press, 1962.

Kahn, H., Brown, W., and Martel, L. *The Next 200 Years.* New York: William Morrow, 1976.

Kane, J. "A Primer for a New Cross-Impact Language — KSIM." *Technological Forecasting and Social Change,* 1972, *4* (2), 129–142.

Nanus, B. "QUEST — Quick Environmental Scanning Technique." *Long Range Planning,* 1982, *15* (2), 39–45.

Toffler, A. *Future Shock.* New York: Random House, 1970.

Von Karman, T. *Towards New Horizons.* Washington, D.C.: Army Air Force Scientific Advisory Group, 1945.

Selwyn Enzer is associate director of the Center for Futures Research, Graduate School of Business Administration, University of Southern California. He is recognized nationally and internationally as one of the pioneers in futures research. His many contributions include the development of the INTERAX model described in this chapter.

Futures techniques may advance the development of institutional research and planning, but they also may change the fundamental nature of these tasks.

Institutional Research and Planning: Is Futures Research The Next Step?

Richard B. Heydinger

The purpose of this chapter is to examine critically the potential uses of futures techniques for institutional research and planning. To accomplish this purpose, it is instructive to trace the important historical forces that have led us to this point in the development of institutional research and planning. In addition, some brief comments on the current status of futures research will aid our review. From this context, we can proceed to review critically the potential of the approaches and ideas presented in this volume.

The Development of Institutional Research

Anyone who has worked for any time in a college or a university probably has outdated images of those staff members who consistently provided up-to-date information on the number of students in the sophomore class or the percentage of freshmen taking introductory chemistry. Such persons

The paper was prepared with the generous support of the W. K. Kellogg Foundation.

J. L. Morrison, W. L. Renfro, and W. I. Boucher (Eds.). *Applying Methods and Techniques of Futures Research.*
New Directions for Institutional Research, no. 39. San Francisco: Jossey-Bass, September 1983.

collected and collated important operational data, and it can be argued that these now seemingly extinct sources of unargued data were the forerunners of the profession we now call institutional research.

Between the two world wars, social science matured as research techniques became more sophisticated, and such fields as psychology and sociology became established academic disciplines. As Jedamus and Peterson point out in the introduction to their institutional research (IR) handbook, "In this period, institutional research had its beginnings, emerging as an outgrowth of educational research at universities such as Minnesota and as a means for measuring and comparing institutional performance, as in the work of John Dale Russell at Chicago" (1980, p. x). This initial stage in the evolution of IR rooted the field strongly in the growing traditions of social science research. At this point, IR professionals typically were faculty members interested in higher education as a topic for study. Perhaps the results of this research found their way into discussions of institutional policies.

With the explosion of higher education in the 1950s and the 1960s, colleges and universities became complex modern organizations occupying a central place on the nation's agenda. Federal and state policy makers found it necessary to have descriptive information on the status of higher education; campus officials found it increasingly difficult to administer their now complex institutions without descriptive as well as analytical information. As a result, an office or a person with appropriate interest or research background was assigned the responsibility of responding to external requests for data and providing central officers with needed operational data. With very little ceremony, institutions established the first offices of institutional research, without knowing precisely what to call these offices and without fully realizing the increasingly important role they would come to occupy in supporting administrations. During this period, institutional research was focused on describing higher education and examining academic program needs. As a profession, institutional research was in its adolescence, making choices between academic research and analytical administrative staff work.

An equally important development during the 1960s was the emergence of higher education as a credentialed field of study. Graduate and research centers were established at Columbia, at Michigan, and at the University of California–Berkeley, propelling the development of institutional research. Armed with research degrees, and often accepting their first positions with responsibilities for institutional research, graduates of these programs began to use increasingly sophisticated social science techniques to study higher education. Although their positions were usually administrative, they viewed themselves as potential scholars and objective researchers. Their work was aimed at studying higher education in support of policy analysis and administrative decision making. This arrangement was consistent with the forces influencing higher education, for decision making was moving from an age of rationalism (the 1960s) to one of empiricism dictated by the conditions and social moods of the 1970s (Norris and Mims, 1983).

During this period, institutional research became a distinct field within higher education administration. IR offices, using modern management information techniques and tools, developed data bases for a wide variety of internal operational measures. More sophisticated offices generated forecasts built from these data.

Today we can characterize institutional research as a relative mature staff function within higher education. In recent years, it has shown a slowing in the pace of its evolution and a refinement of the techniques it proposed in the 1960s and the 1970s. The purposes of institutional research seem to be clear, as defined in a recent treatise on the topic (Saupe, 1981): "research conducted within an institution of higher education in order to provide information which *supports* institutional planning, policy formulation, and decision making" (p. 1; emphasis added). A panel of past AIR presidents at the 1980 Association for Institutional Research forum reinforced the importance of maintaining the objective stance of true researchers: "But we should not define our work as policy formulation, as decision making, or as planning, or else we will forget that our responsibility is research and will forget what is the fundamental nature of research" (Past Presidents' Panel, 1980, p. 33). Yet in this same discussion, the fundamental dilemma facing institutional research during this decade was also presented: "With increased technology and increased professionalism, this group has developed into one which has had a significant impact on both the direction of institutional decisions and on the quality of the institutional decision-making process. However, with greater statewide coordination and federal reporting requirements, coupled with the feeling of some that institutional researchers are too pure to get involved in the implementation phase of planning or too scholarly to become involved in politics, institutional researchers run the risk of again becoming only data providers" (p. 34).

As the discussion below will show, the question of the posture of institutional researchers within college or university administrations has direct bearing on our critique of the utility of futures methodologies.

The Evolution of Planning

A second factor to consider in this critique is the state of the art of higher education planning. Organizational planning has developed in a time frame parallel to that of institutional research, and like IR, it has proceeded through distinct stages. (Although this discussion treats these developments as separate topics, they are not unrelated.)

Planning has advanced through four successive stages, with each succeeding stage building on the strengths of the former while advancing the field to overcome its weaknesses. Originally, organizational planning was not viewed as a discrete activity, but was subsumed under the annual budgeting process. Each year, as revenue and expense projections were drawn up, decision makers considered directional changes to be made. Although technological, social, and political trends were weighed, the future was projected almost exclusively in economic and quantitative terms. Using this set of financial practices as the primary vehicle for addressing the future, organizational planning was in its first stage: annual budgeting.

As people recognized the shortcomings of this exclusively financial perspective and organizations began to specify their purposes in detail, organizational planning moved into its second stage: specification of goals and objectives. This stage expanded vision beyond the time frame of a single year. Simultaneously, society's needs for quantification and accountability grew. Not surprisingly, the specification of institutional goals and objectives became one standard against which success could be measured. Organizations realized that there was a cause-and-effect relationship between specifying a future and marshalling resources to move toward this vision.

With the advent of computing and our tremendously increased capabilities for storing and manipulating quantitative information, organizations moved to a third stage of planning: forecasting. On the basis of combining quantitative, historical records of companies with predictions about external forces, it became possible to develop mathematical models to forecast the future of organizations. As our understanding of the world's interrelationships grew, our confidence in our ability to predict the future also grew. Of course, the quantifiable and the measurable were most easily forecast. Social, political, and technological trends were also considered, but they were difficult if not impossible to include in point-specific forecasts.

Although we had vastly improved our vision and our capabilities for dealing with the "futurity" of our decisions (Drucker, 1973, p. 125), twenty years of experience with planning revealed the seemingly obvious fact that the future is unpredictable. We became increasingly aware that our organizations exist within an open system of interactions so complex and so dynamic that a new format for planning was called for. This format would build on the strengths of the previous stages of planning: the necessity of the budget cycle, the effectiveness of specifying organizational intentions, and the usefulness of examining quantitative projections. Nevertheless, it had to recognize the uncertainty of the future while simultaneously preparing the organization to react to a wide range of possibilities. Moreover, the new methodology had to be sensitive to the influence of the external environment on the organization itself.

From this set of needs, organizational planning moved into its fourth and current stage: strategic planning. Fundamentally, there are four aspects of strategic planning: setting goals, understanding the environment, developing strategies, and agreeing on a plan. It is beyond the scope of this chapter to discuss each of these aspects in detail, but realizing the important position the environment occupies in effective organizational planning is central to our critique of futures techniques.

Strategic planning, more than any of the previous stages of planning, takes cognizance of forces that are external to the organization, and which can potentially affect the organization's attainment of its goals. Because this view is the newest component of strategic planning, environmental assessment techniques are still evolving, such that today there is little agreement even on terminology. Nevertheless, the recognition of the key role that external forces play is an important development in organizational planning.

A second and related dimension that strategic planning brings to the fore is the recognition of uncertainty. Thus, strategic planning has eschewed the single future in favor of presenting a range of possible conditions. It builds on the recognition that the future is unpredictable. It then moves to encompass a wide range of possible external conditions, not just the most probable. Similarly, it seeks to broaden the number and types of strategies planners consider.

Today's up-to-date institutional researcher, who is requested to support the planning process, has an expanded set of responsibilities to consider. Not only must data be collected about the internal workings of an institution; data sets that produce environmental scans may also be considered to be within IR's purview. We shall want to consider this point when we return to our detailed critique of futures techniques.

Futures Research: A Controversial Field

Perhaps no academic field sparks more controversy among academicians than the field of futures research. The hyperbole in this debate is captured in the following excerpts, all taken from an excellent chapter on futures techniques by Kirschling and Huckfeldt in Jedamus's (1980) handbook. First, in support of futures studies: "McLuhan suggests that we are traveling down a super highway at 100 miles an hour with our eyes fixed on the rear view mirror" (p. 204). With his usual flair John Silber pokes fun at futurism: "The educators of 1976 peered into the future through an opening flanked by two immense figures. Standing like the pillars of Hercules, Herman Kahn and Colonel Blimp symbolized the durability inherent in planning—pretension and error" (p. 207). Jay Mendell, a noted futurist, counters: "Tunnel vision and shortsightedness, carefully managed and nurtured, have in the past been positive, not negative, in propelling executives to the top" (p. 207).

Regardless of one's position in this debate, there is little doubt that futurism has captured the imaginations of noted and respected people in our society. As only one of many examples that can be cited, in 1982 the U.S. House of Representatives Committee on Energy and Commerce (1983) held detailed hearings on approaches and techniques for establishing public-issue early warning systems. Testimony was taken from many noted futurists and strategic corporate planners who have pioneered many of the techniques discussed in this volume.

In reviewing these techniques, it is advisable to transcend the emotionalism that plagues the field of futurism and, as objectively as possible, assess each technique for its applicability to and utility within particular institutions. Given the challenges facing higher education, information must accurately assess institutions and their options. Perhaps even more important, institutions will be best served if those responsible for decision making are helped to consider the broadest possible set of alternatives. Futurism offers a number of responses to institutions' needs, but are these responses applicable to institutional research and planning in higher education today?

Institutional Research at the Crossroads

The developments traced above are stretching the role of the institutional researcher. As planning has assumed an increasingly important role in higher education, offices of institutional research are frequently asked to assume responsibility for managing institutional planning processes. This development has led to debate on differentiating the roles of planning and institutional research. As noted earlier, institutional research is conducted in support of planning, policy formulation, and decision making. Most traditional institutional researchers would argue that institutional research is objective analysis that investigates and lays out alternative courses of action for decision makers, and that it may compromise itself if it becomes involved in the decision making process.

In contrast, planning is the essence of decision making. It cannot be objective, for within the planning process, value conflicts must be resolved, strategies must be agreed upon, and resources must be allocated. The effective planning staff member may propose new decision-making methods (such as those outlined in this volume), challenge the conclusions of IR studies, advocate a particular recommendation, and assist in the implementation of decisions. When compared to the more classic definition of institutional research, these responsibilities go beyond the role of IR.

Thus, as institutional researchers become directly involved in the planning enterprise, they assume a second and perhaps distinct role. This new role and its contrasting needs with institutional research cannot be overlooked as we evaluate the utility of futures techniques.

Yet, in reality, these distinctions cannot be drawn as precisely as they are here. Sidney Suslow (1972) has discussed the role of institutional research and the dilemma the planning process poses for researchers. Although his language conveys the attitudes of the period, in these lengthy citations Suslow conveys some important distinctions that are fundamental to our review of futures techniques.

> To study and to evaluate are roles quite distinct from ones which determine and decide, but the dichotomy for institutional research can be a viable one if the latter two roles are carefully delineated. Institutional research can help identify and gain consensus on issues and problems faced by the institution if it assists the policy formulation process by specifying feasible actions with respect to the issues and problems and if it analyzes the probable utilities and disutilities of each action.
>
> There should be no dilemma for the individual practitioner of institutional research who is concerned with involvement in policy formulation; for, if evaluations have been achieved through objective study and research, the practitioner should feel free to state a preference for one alternative over another either independently or when called upon to do so by another agency. Extensive or continuous participation in policy formulation will negate the primary role of the institutional researcher, although neither specific guidelines nor any clearly defined boundaries are available to him to judge when his role has ceased to be institutional research and has become entirely different. The institutional research practitioner is not, per se, an administrator; and, if his work within his own institution is to be accepted without suspicion or hostility, he must not act in such a way as to preempt or appear to preempt the prerogatives of the administrators. On the other hand, it also must be stressed that the administrator is not, per se, a researcher. The researcher who has been scrupulous in developing a set of options for final evaluation and decision, allowing for points of view and evaluations other than his own, has been as objective as is humanly possible. His subsequent participation in the administrative process need not impair the rational quality of his initial contribution at the research stage. Whenever that participation becomes more or less continuous and goal-directed, the researcher role has been vacated and the administrator role is dominant [Suslow, 1972, pp. 5–6].

Planning and evaluation are not synonymous terms. More critically, they are often incompatible activities or attitudes. Institutional research is primarily evaluation, but if it is to achieve the fundamental goal of enhancing academic and administrative processes, it must work closely with institutional agencies which have institutionwide responsibility for planning and policy formulation. Contemporary planning in most colleges and universities entails coordination and integration of all aspects of planning — academic, physical, and financial — and one of the chief functions of institutional research is to contribute to this coordination and integration. These contributions may take various forms, such as prognostications, simulations, models, and explorations, and the individual researcher may be called upon to play an active role in the whole planning process; however, as with the problem of administration versus research discussed in preceding pages, institutional research diminishes to the extent that it becomes involved in the implementation of academic plans. The difficulty for some researchers is their inability to extricate themselves at the proper stage of the planning process.... Unless the researcher stops short of implementation in the planning process, he relinquishes his influence as an objective evaluator and he assumes a partisan role [p. 14–15].

To assess the utility of futures techniques, it is important that readers — whether IR professionals, planning staff members, or both — have their roles clearly in mind, both in terms of current definition and in terms of the changes they would like to introduce. In summary, the distinctions being drawn here are aptly conveyed by Sheehan (1982), who envisions a simple, one-dimensional chart (see Figure 1). Institutional researchers and planning staff members must ask themselves where, in the context of their own institutions, they see their roles on Sheehan's continuum.

Futures Techniques and the IR and Planning Functions

Consistent with the distinctions drawn above, the futures approaches presented in this volume can be grouped into two categories. The chapters on environmental scanning, and multiple scenario analysis present methods for collecting data on the external environment. The chapters that discuss

Figure 1. Distinctions Between Staff Roles

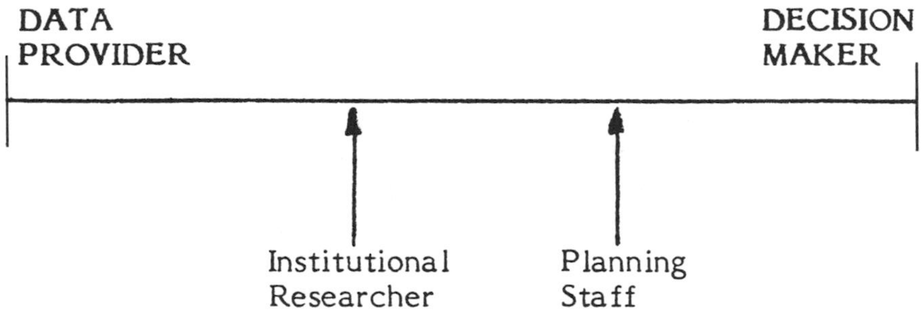

DATA
PROVIDER

DECISION
MAKER

Institutional
Researcher

Planning
Staff

"futuring" and cross-impact analysis present techniques for aiding and expanding decision-making processes. The external data methodologies can be viewed as supporting the traditional institutional research function, whereas the decision aids are more consistent with the roles of planning staff members.

External Data Methodologies

There can be little doubt that higher education has significantly expanded its institutional research and planning capabilities over the past decades, but the challenges facing higher education call for new, more sophisticated and more comprehensive environmental sensors (see Enzer's chapter in this volume).

Change may be occurring at such a quickened pace that organizations as large and as overcommitted as colleges and universities need a finely tuned process to alert them to the threats and opportunities coalescing on the horizon. Consider, for example, how different the strains and tribulations of higher education might have been in the 1970s if institutions had been forewarned of changes in women's attitudes toward careers and of their demand for postgraduate study. Some institutions possibly could have avoided costly and emotional court fights. In contrast, institutions that anticipated society's growing concern with increases in the older proportion of our population have had the years necessary to develop high-quality gerontology programs so that they are in place today as this need comes to the top of society's agenda.

If an IR office decides that a comprehensive, continuous environmental scanning operation is needed, important questions must be addressed. Who really wants this information? Many decision makers see such data as extraneous to the day-to-day decisions. And what methodology will be used? There are many approaches to accumulating such information, most of which are more art than science. For example, The Naisbitt Group bases its environmental scanning services on a content analysis methodology, which uses the construct of the "news hole" in local newspapers (Naisbitt, 1982, pp. 3–4). The Trend Analysis Program conducted by the American Council of Life Insurance abstracts from many different types of publications, and then a steering committee creates the actual scan. In any case, it is important to anticipate the time and energy that will be required for sifting through massive amounts of literature and data.

In considering options for collecting environmental data, a number of possibilities should be evaluated. Basic environmental trends facing colleges and universities may not be markedly different from those affecting other higher educational institutions. Perhaps it will make sense to collaborate on regional environmental monitoring programs. Similarly, we must decide whether to monitor only trends affecting a region or also to keep abreast of all major developments around the United States and worldwide. Cursory review of the national environmental scanning data provided by commercial services shows that these data provide clues to factors that should be monitored, but that they do not necessarily call attention to important issues in particular regions. Perhaps a regional scanning approach is best after all.

It also seems advisable to consider the possibility of "piggybacking" on existing resources. Certainly, an IR office should not be making its own projections of the region's economy, nor do higher education institutions have the resources to subscribe to sophisticated services. Neighboring private corporations may be willing to offer some assistance. Many large corporations have given responsibility for scanning to particular offices or individuals. Sometimes scanning is done in public affairs or corporate relations offices or in the corporate strategic planning offices. Such offices often subscribe to one or more national scanning services. Their expertise in selected areas (for example, economy, technology) can complement the expertise of the institution. Of course, colleges and universities should not overlook the wealth of expertise they have in their own faculties. The irony of higher education scanning operations is that private corporations hire our faculty members to provide forecasts, while administrators overlook these valuable sources of information.

The most effective scanning operations are interdisciplinary. Hence, as offices of institutional research become involved in scanning, they must ask themselves if they have the necessary breadth to do the job effectively.

The question of when and how to begin an environmental scanning process can be immobilizing. For example, for nearly eighteen months the University of Minnesota has been trying to determine the best way to establish a formal environmental scanning process: Should it be heavily data- and report-oriented, or should it concentrate on conducting a series of seminars in which the central officers would discuss a single longer-range issue? With too many questions unresolved and an unclear demand for the product, we are only now making a decision on the best way to proceed. George Keller (1983) offers some particularly sage advice, which we should have heeded: "It is a common flaw among the highly learned in academe to prefer to do very little until near-certainty and rigorous methodologies have been worked out. But life does not allow such delays. We must act, doing the best we can with what we have. Herodotus and Thucydides wrote the first histories without a tidy method. Environmental scanning, too, should proceed regardless, adjusting regularly to new conditions" (p. 158).

Delphi is a method for collecting subjective data on the external environment. This technique can form the basis of additional scanning or can even produce the scan itself. QUEST is a scanning approach that builds on the knowledge of an organization's decision makers. It is an efficient process that may alter the role of institutional researchers, but does not necessarily require the same effort as the other scanning techniques. (See Enzer's chapter in this volume.)

Each of these approaches forces institutions to consider systematically the possible consequences of external trends and events. The judgmental techniques, which lack a rigorous theoretical base, are built on some arguable assumptions about people's capabilities for meaningful futures analysis. Nevertheless, the process of systematically examining future trends from the varied perspectives of an interdisciplinary team will expand the number of possibilities to be considered.

How should scanning information be used in planning? Multiple scenario analysis (MSA) offers a useful vehicle for indirectly informing planners at all levels about environmental trends and potentially important events. As different sets of premises are presented for the same environmental factors, MSA reminds us of the future's unpredictability.

Both multiple scenario analysis and environmental scanning present options that should at least be considered by any office of institutional research or planning that is seeking to expand institutional awareness of influences from the external environment. These techniques expand the capabilities and the data bases of the office of institutional research, but they do not alter its fundamental role as a support for policy analysis and decision making. Employing these techniques does not change the objective role that some would argue institutional researchers must maintain if they are to support institutional development most effectively. It also can be argued that including external data and environmental scanning techniques may make the next significant evolutionary step for institutional research.

Decision Aids

The second group of techniques presented in this volume stands in marked contrast to the external data methodologies discussed above. Futures techniques such as the cross-impact matrix, the futures wheel, and even some uses of the Delphi are basically group processing techniques. Although their focus is on tapping our knowledge and expanding our thinking with regard to the future, they are not data collection or analysis techniques, as commonly defined by institutional researchers. Instead, they are appropriately categorized as a specialized subset of the literally hundreds of group processing techniques. Techniques familiar to a large number of people, but not limited to a focus on the future, include brainstorming, values voting, and creative problem solving. Viewing this set of futures methods as a subset of group processing techniques highlights the important shift in role that use of these techniques will have for traditional institutional research offices. If IR is viewed exclusively as research in support of planning, policy formation, and decision making, then it can be argued that these techniques fall outside the scope of IR. (Of course, we should not overlook their utility in managing an office of institutional research, but these techniques do not directly contribute to the institutional research function, as it is classically defined.)

Still, these approaches cannot be dismissed so easily, for they offer higher education some useful contemporary tools. There is little need to restate here the conditions facing higher education; many of the forces at work are summarized in the editors' introduction to this volume. It is important, however, to note the tortuous course many institutions are taking in adapting to the future. For example, consider how many schools of library science and education are under fire, how many institutions are rushing to establish evening and weekend business programs, and how many research universities are working feverishly to establish a corporate–university research relationship. Is this the result of strategic planning built on a careful exploration of future alternatives, or does it follow the path of least resistance and mimic the conclusions of peer institutions? Is it avoidance of the big issues that can alter the fundamental characteristics of higher education?

George Keller (1983) tells us that a new form of decision making is slowly infiltrating higher education: strategic management. Although positive change is occurring, Keller states confidently that higher education could benefit from expanded vision and a more formal exploration of alternative futures. Group processing techniques offer some modest vehicles for this trip; but they are planning aids, not institutional research aids.

More than most industries, higher education administration seems to be limited by its own approaches to decision making. It is fascinating to note the seeming willingness of many private corporations to test new techniques for decision making. For example, technique books are frequently on the best-selling lists of management books, and many organizational development consultants support their operations by the development of new techniques, but higher education seems reluctant to test such new decision-making and planning aids as the futures wheel or the cross-impact matrix. Frequently, these techniques are dismissed as gimmicks of the futurists. Such reactions only reduce the possibility of improving higher education.

As institutions move increasingly toward strategic planning and management, these techniques should be made available. They must be used carefully when the situation calls for them, not mindlessly introduced simply to ensure that we are up to date. Six guidelines can be offered for using these approaches:

1. Do not underestimate the feeling of risk you will experience when suggesting such new approaches.
2. Do not overlook the impact that the use of such techniques can have on your credibility within the institution. Successful use of a new

approach may call attention to your value to the institution, but failure may result in branding you a futurist (as some would say, a sure path to ignominy).

3. Recognize that you are now playing the role of an in-house organizational development consultant. This is not necessarily inadvisable, but it may affect people's perceptions of your other roles.

4. Do not label techniques by announcing, "Well, how about trying a futures wheel?" This only produces resistance, which often can be avoided by first describing the decision-making problem you are facing and then suggesting the steps (not the name of the techniques) that may assist the group's deliberations.

5. Do not slavishly follow the steps of a technique if they do not naturally conform to the direction in which the group is headed. Modify the approach to the task at hand.

6. Before using any of these approaches, think through all the steps. Put yourself in the place of a participant, and guarantee that the questions are sensible and the judgments required can be made in the time allotted.

The critical stance taken in this chapter is not intended to dissuade readers from using futures techniques. In fact, this author firmly supports the use of a wide range of group processing techniques to aid planning and decision making and has used them, both successfully and unsuccessfully, on many occasions. Rather, this critical review is offered to increase the likelihood that these techniques will be used effectively at the start and, hence, in the future.

This entire cluster of planning approaches rests on two fundamental building blocks. First, they systematically expand the options under consideration and then seek to collate these alternatives into an agenda for action. The danger is always that they will provide intellectual grist without an "action residue of shared visions, policies, and plans" (Kirschling and Huckfeldt, 1980, p. 208). Second, they build on the wealth of information most higher education administrators have about their institutions as well as about society. They recognize the capability of the human brain to integrate this information, and they rely on human judgment to breathe meaning into these data. These processes go beyond rational models of planning. Drucker tells us that strategic planning techniques are not intended to eliminate judgment or to replace hunches; they are intended to strengthen and expand them (1973, p. 129).

Futurism and Higher Education Administration

In the past two years, higher education has rushed into the future. Unforeseen financial conditions are facing all public institutions, and a long-awaited enrollment decline is upon us. Except for a few optimistic voices in the wilderness (Bowen, 1982), the industry is suffering from a crisis of confidence.

If we are to respond creatively, we must begin to look beyond our own organizational boundaries and anticipate internal changes brought on by changing external conditions. We must then take our early warning signals, combine them with our existing internal data and forecasting techniques, and ensure that we tap the wealth of creativity and resourcefulness higher education has to offer. As Suslow noted over ten years ago, "No single or simple combination of disciplines provides sufficient knowledge to analyze the effectiveness of universities and colleges in a systematic and critical manner.... The quality of the institutional researcher lies in his ability to discern which methodologies are appropriate to the problem with which he is concerned" (1972, p. 1). New techniques and data collection methodologies can be invaluable aids in this process, but they can never replace the need for creative insight, organizational savvy, and a willingness to take risks.

References

Association for Institutional Research. "Past Presidents' Panel: AIR in the Eighties." In P. J. Staskey (Ed.), *Issues for the Eighties: Proceedings*. Tallahassee: Association for Institutional Research, 1980.

Bowen, H. *The State of the Nation and the Agenda for Higher Education*. San Francisco: Jossey-Bass, 1982.

Drucker, P. F. *Management: Tasks, Responsibilities, Practices*. New York: Harper & Row, 1973.

Jedamus, P., and Peterson, M. W. *Improving Academic Management*. San Francisco: Jossey-Bass, 1980.

Keller, G. *Academic Strategy*. Baltimore: The Johns Hopkins Press, 1983.

Kirschling, W., and Huckfeldt, V. "Projecting Alternative Futures." In P. Jedamus (Ed.), *Improving Academic Management*. San Francisco: Jossey-Bass, 1980.

Naisbitt, J. *Megatrends*. New York: Warner Books, 1982.

Norris, D. M., and Mims, R. S. "A New Maturity for Institutional Planning and Information Management." Unpublished paper, 1983.

Saupe, J. *The Functions of Institutional Research*. Tallahassee: Association for Institutional Research, 1981.

Sheehan, B. Personal correspondence, July 16, 1982.

Suslow, S. *A Declaration on Institutional Research*. Tallahassee: Association for Institutional Research, 1972.

United States House of Representatives Committee on Energy and Commerce. *Public-Issue Early Warning Systems: Legislative and Institutional Alternatives*. Washington, D.C.: U.S. Government Printing Office, 1983.

Richard B. Heydinger is assistant to the vice-president for academic affairs at the University of Minnesota. He was also selected as a Kellogg National Fellow to study strategic planning and the future of higher education.

This chapter contains a selection of twenty-one works concerned with methods of futures research.

Selected Bibliography

Wayne I. Boucher

The literature of futures research is enormous, in part because the field itself can now look back on some twenty years of work to define its philosophy, methods, successes, and failures. The literature is extensive also because much of it has been self-published by think tanks, government agencies, academic research centers, and so forth, and efforts at quality control have often been feeble. Moreover, much of the literature involves ritualistic incantation of the same ideas, instead of the reporting or assessment of new ones. As Dror (1973) put the matter ten years ago, "Read three main books in methodology, read a dozen books of substantive ideas on the future, and look over the proceedings of the Kyoto Conference [on futures research, held in Japan in 1970] — and you have got it all! . . . Clearly, the urgent need is for innovative work, new ideas, better methodologies, new designs, rather than for sharing and resharing what has already been shared several times over" (p. 111). Little has changed since Dror wrote these words, although (as the present volume attempts to show) it is clear that futures research has already entered a period of deep self-examination and probable redirection. Where this redirection may lead is not entirely certain, of course, but there is reason to believe that various long-overdue changes, as well as some surprising innovations, are in store.

For readers interested in learning more about futures research as it stands today, a guide to the literature can be brief — especially to the literature

J. L. Morrison, W. L. Renfro, and W. I. Boucher (Eds.). *Applying Methods and Techniques of Futures Research.*
New Directions for Institutional Research, no. 39. San Francisco: Jossey-Bass, September 1983.

principally on methodologies. The following twenty-one items should provide a rich enough choice. They range from the introductory to the fairly technical, but none is particularly mathematical, and virtually all tend to be directed toward managers, as well as toward analysts and planners.

Incidentally, the phrase *technological forecasting* appears in the titles of a number of these works, a reflection of the fact that many practitioners of futures research began by forecasting the likely evolution of physical technologies. Nevertheless, all these publications are directly relevant to—indeed, descriptive of—futures research. Although the authors' examples are usually drawn from research and development and from environmental impact analysis, the imaginative reader should have little difficulty in substituting examples from educational policy planning and administration. The same is true for publications prepared for corporate or governmental audiences; the point is that the methods of futures research are perfectly general and the essential condition for their application is uncertainty about possible futures.

Armstrong, J. S. *Long-Range Forecasting.* New York: Wiley, 1978.

Often glib, this book is nevertheless quite valuable in its discussions of various standard forecasting techniques, with explicit reference to major research findings on these techniques. But the author's main criterion for evaluating these techniques is their predictive accuracy, and the discussion of the techniques of futures research is either superficial (Delphi, scenario writing) or nonexistent (cross-impact analysis). Contains an extensive bibliography.

Asher, W. *Forecasting: An Appraisal for Policy Makers and Planners.* Baltimore: The Johns Hopkins University Press, 1978.

A very perceptive review of the nature and accuracy of techniques used in demographic, economic, energy, transportation, and technological forecasting. A major contribution to forecasting and futures research, despite the author's insistence that accuracy must be the principal basis for evaluation.

Ayres, R. V. *Technological Forecasting and Long-Range Planning.* New York: McGraw-Hill, 1969.

The first four chapters of this book are still one of the best introductory statements on forecasting. Later chapters deal primarily with methodology and are strong on mathematical techniques, but very weak on qualitative-judgmental methods.

Boucher, W. I. (Ed.). *The Study of the Future: An Agenda for Research.* Washington, D.C.: U.S. Government Printing Office, 1977.

This anthology surveys the entire field of futures research — basic concepts, methods, areas of application, and institutionalization — and evaluates a large set of proposed research efforts to improve the art and science of forecasting. Since no important work has been accomplished in the last few years on any of the top-ranked projects on the agenda, this volume remains a good description of the state of the art. Contains an extensive bibliography.

Duncan, O. D. "Social Forecasting — The State of the Art." *The Public Interest,* 1973, *17,* 88–118.

An intelligent discussion of the strengths, weaknesses, pitfalls, and limitations of forecasters and forecasting. This paper remains quite current despite the years since its publication.

Enzer, S. "A Case Study Using Forecasting as a Decision-Making Aid." *Futures,* 1970, *4,* 341–362.

Enzer was the first researcher to combine formally the use of futures research techniques, such as Delphi and cross-impact analysis, in a workshop setting to illustrate how a group could tackle a typical futures problem and see how these techniques supported both the deliberations and each other. This work directly inspired later approaches designed not to illustrate the methods but to provide a vehicle for actually preparing forecasts and evaluating policy alternatives. (Among these more recent approaches are the CONSENSOR-based meeting, the Focused Planning Effort, and QUEST). This early paper is a useful introduction to the idea of futures workshops.

Enzer, S. "INTERAX — An Interactive Model for Studying Future Business Environments: Parts I and II." *Technological Forecasting and Social Change,* 1980, *17,* 141–159, 211–242.

Enzer's work on cross-impact analysis defines the state of the art. This two-part paper provides a good introduction to the research, particularly to the INTERAX (interactive cross-impact simulation) model, which generates scenarios and allows the user to interact with on-folding individual futures to explore a variety of strategic issues.

Fowles, J. (Ed.). *Handbook of Futures Research.* Westport, Conn.: Greenwood Press, 1978.

Part III of this anthology contains a dozen articles on the techniques of futures research. Unfortunately, some of these articles tend to ignore important relevant work by others and hence are not fully descriptive of the state of the art. If read as personal statements on the methods, however, these articles can be of value.

Helmer, O., and Rescher, N. "On the Epistemology of the Inexact Sciences." *Management Science,* 1959, *1,* 25–52.

A basic statement on the place, role, and value of expert opinion and conjecture in forecasting and futures research.

Hencley, S. P., and Yates, J. R. (Eds.). *Futurism in Education: Methodologies.* Berkeley, Calif.: McCutchan, 1974.

One of the better anthologies on the methods of forecasting and futures research, this book is still worth consulting.

Jantsch, E. *Technological Forecasting in Perspective.* Paris: Organization for Economic Cooperation and Development, 1976.

The first authoritative and comprehensive treatment of the state of the art of modern forecasting methods. Sometimes very heavy reading, but still valuable. Contains an extensive bibliography.

Jones, J., and Twiss, B. *Forecasting Technology for Planning Decisions.* New York: Petrocelli, 1978.

Although dated in its discussion of some forecasting methods, this book provides a good introduction to forecasting and futures research. Written in plain English, it draws both on American and European experience in its examples (mainly corporate), emphasizing the pragmatic.

Kahn, H., and Wiener, A. *The Year 2000.* New York: Macmillan, 1967.

Kahn is widely recognized as a pioneer in the development of scenario writing in futures studies. Most of his other books also devote considerable space to this technique, but the discussion in the pages of *The Year 2000* is an excellent place to begin.

Kahneman, D., Slovic, P., and Tversky, A. *Judgment Under Uncertainty: Heuristics and Biases.* New York: Cambridge University Press, 1982.

This is an important collection of papers concerned with the ways in which people judge uncertain events. Since the ability to do this job well is fundamental to futures research, and since these papers indicate the considerable human weaknesses involved in making judgments, this book makes a powerful case for modesty in claims about futures studies. This is assuredly not an introductory-level book, but it should be examined once the reader is familiar with the basic techniques of futures research. Contains an extensive bibliography.

Linstone, H. A., and Turoff, M. (Eds.). *The Delphi Method: Techniques and Application.* Reading, Mass.: Addison-Wesley, 1975.

This anthology brings together many important papers on Delphi; it also attempts to cover cross-impact analysis. The volume remains the only book-length treatment of Delphi, apart from Harold Sackman's (1975) highly critical and often misguided *Delphi Critique.* Contains an extensive bibliography.

Linstone, H. A., Simmonds, W. H. (Eds.). *Futures Research: New Directions.* Reading, Mass.: Addison-Wesley, 1977.

A number of these papers argue that, in the editor's words, "we must move beyond the objective, analytic, reductionist, number-oriented, optimizing, and fail-safe approach to futures problems and learn to think with equal fluency in more subjective, synthesizing, holistic, qualitative, option-increasing safe-fail ways." This statement may seem trendy, if not extreme, but at least the editors tone it down in their epilogue, where they say that "the thrust is toward a *balance* between the two sets of attributes, not a replacement of one set by the other."

Martino, J. P. *Technological Forecasting for Decision Making.* (2nd ed.) New York: Elsevier Scientific Publishing Company, 1983.

The first edition of this book (1972) was generally recognized as a major contribution to the fields of forecasting and futures research. It not only synthesized much of what was then known about available methods of forecasting but also provided an authoritative discussion of philosphical issues, practical questions, and problems of evaluation and implementation. The new edition updates the original, adding new examples of applications and extending the discussion of computer models.

Meadows, D. H., Meadows, D. L., Randers, J., and Behrens, W. W., III. *The Limits to Growth.* New York: Universe Books, 1972.

A painless way to learn about system dynamics. More demanding discussions will be found in books by Jay Forrester (1971), Dennis and Donella Meadows (1973), and Mesarovic and Pestel (1974).

Porter, A. L. *A Guidebook for Technology Assessment and Impact Analysis.* New York: Elsevier Science Publishing Company, 1980.

This book is a comprehensive, well-organized discussion of technology assessment, an offshoot of futures research that came into vogue in the late 1960s. Well behind the state of the art at the time of its publication, this book is nevertheless valuable in its careful pragmatic discussion of how and why to conduct a futures analysis. Contains an extensive bibliography.

Quade, E. S. *Analysis for Public Decisions*. New York: American Elsevier, 1975.

A good discussion, by a distinguished RAND Corporation specialist, of the philosophy and methods of systems analysis. Because futures research grew out of systems analysis — and, indeed, is essentially only a special emphasis within systems analysis — this book can serve as a most informative guide to understanding the intellectual context of futures research.

Renfro, W. L. *The Legislative Role of Corporations*. New York: American Management Associations, 1983.

A thorough exploration of the development cycle of public issues from changing social values to final federal regulations. This book describes the congressional process as it is working today as well as how it is changing in the future. It provides a good guide to scanning emerging legislative issues.

Shane, H. G. "Future-Planning as a Means of Shaping Educational Change." In *The Curriculum: Retrospect and Prospect*. Chicago: The National Society for the Study of Education, 1971.

An early but still relevant statement on the potential contributions of futures research to the educational policy process. Written by an educator who is well known for his efforts to infuse a futures orientation into education.

Additional Sources

Edrich, H. "Keeping a Weather Eye on the Future." *Planning Reivew,* January 1980, 11–14.

Ewing, R. P. "The Uses of Futurist Techniques in Issues Management." *Public Relations Quarterly,* Winter 1979, 15–19.

Godiwalla, Y. "Environmental Scanning — Does It Help the Chief Executive?" *Long Range Planning,* October 1980, 87–99.

Hegarty, W. H. "Strategic Planning in the 1980s — Coping with Complex External Forces." *Planning Review,* 1981, *40,* 8–12, 40.

Kast, F. "Scanning the Future Environment: Social Indicators." *California Management Review,* Fall 1980, 22–32.

Klein, H. E., and Linneman, R. "The Use of Scenarios in Corporate Planning — Eight Case Histories." *Long Range Planning,* 1981, *14,* 49–77.

Klein, H. E., and Newman, W. H. "How to Integrate New Environmental Forces into Strategic Planning." *Management Review,* July 1980, 40–48.

Lanford, H. W. *Technological Forecasting Methodologies: A Synthesis*. New York: American Management Association, 1972.

Linneman, R. E., and Klein, H. E. "The Use of Multiple Scenarios by U.S. Industrial Companies." *Long Range Planning,* 1979, *12,* 83–90.

MacNulty, C. A. R. "Scenario Development for Corporate Planning." *Futures,* 1977, *9* (2), 128–138.

Michael, D. *On Learning to Plan and Planning to Learn.* San Francisco: Jossey-Bass, 1973.

Preble, J. F. "Corporate Use of Environmental Scanning." *University of Michigan Business Review,* September 1978, 121–127.

Terry, P. T. "Mechanisms for Environmental Scanning." *Long Range Planning,* June 1977, 2–9.

Vanderwicken, P. "'Externalysis': A New Dimension in Planning." *Planning Review,* July 1982, *45,* 24–27.

Weiner, E. "Future Scanning for Trade Groups and Companies." *Harvard Business Review,* September/October 1976.

Whitehead, A. N. "On Foresight." In W. B. Donham (Ed.). *Business Adrift.* New York: McGraw-Hill, 1931.

References

Dror, Y. "A Third Look at Futures Studies." *Technological Forecasting and Social Change,* 1973, *5* (2), 111.

Forrester, J. *World Dynamics.* Cambridge, Mass.: Wright-Allen, 1971.

Meadows, D. H., and Meadows, D. L. (Eds.). *Toward Global Equilibrium.* New York: Wright-Allen, 1973.

Mesarovic, M., and Pestel, E. *Mankind at the Turning Point.* New York: Dutton, 1974.

Sackman, H. *Delphi Critique.* Lexington, Mass.: Heath, 1975.

Wayne I. Boucher is senior research associate at the Center for Futures Research of the Graduate School of Business Administration, University of Southern California.

Index